D1613032

PRIVACY AND HUMAN RIGHTS

PRIVACY AND HUMAN RIGHTS

AN INTERNATIONAL AND COMPARATIVE STUDY, WITH SPECIAL REFERENCE TO DEVELOPMENTS IN INFORMATION TECHNOLOGY

JAMES MICHAEL

Dartmouth

UNESCO
Publishing

Published jointly by the United Nations
Educational, Scientific and Cultural Organization
7 Place de Fontenoy, 75700 Paris, France

and

Dartmouth Publishing Company Limited
Gower House, Croft Road, Aldershot, Hampshire GU11 3HR,
England

British Library Cataloguing in Publication Data
Michael, James
  Privacy and Human Rights: International
  and Comparative Study, with Special
  Reference to Developments in Information
  Technology
  I. Title
  323.448

Library of Congress Cataloging-in-Publication Data
Michael, James.
    Privacy and human rights : an international and comparative study,
  with special reference to developments in information technology /
  James Michael.
      p.   cm.
    Includes index.
    ISBN 1-85521-381-8 : $57.95 (approx.)
    1. Privacy, Right of.   2. Data protection–Law and legislation.
  3. Human rights.   4. Information technology.   I. Title.
  K3263.M53   1994
  342'.0858–dc20
  [342.2858]   94–11932
                                                                          CIP

Dartmouth ISBN 1 85521 381 8
UNESCO   ISBN 92-3-102808-1

Printed and bound in Great Britain by
Biddles Ltd, Guildford and King's Lynn

Contents

Preface

UNESCO's interest in the area of privacy and personal data protection dates back to 1970. UNESCO had then entrusted the International Commission of Jurists (Geneva) with the preparation of a comparative international study which was published in UNESCO's quarterly *International Social Science Journal* (vol. XXIV, no. 3, 1972) under the title 'The Protection of Privacy'.

In the mid-1980s, UNESCO requested the International Commission of Jurists to update and expand this study. Since 1970, many more Member States had recognized the need to adopt specific legislation in this field (or to enforce existing domestic laws) which took into account the growing computerized processing of such information. In this respect several countries had also established supervisory or monitoring institutions or mechanisms. New problems had also arisen, in particular in relation to transborder data flows. In addition, several international intergovernmental organizations had adopted normative instruments aimed at the protection of personal data, in particular the United Nations, the Commission of the European Communities (EEC), the Council of Europe and the Organization for Economic Co-operation and Development (OECD). This updated study was undertaken by the late Paul Sieghart, then Chairperson of the Executive Committee of Justice, the British section of the International Commission of Jurists.

The purpose of updating this study was twofold: on the one hand, to review the progress achieved through legislation to implement effective protection of privacy, and on the other, to assess the potential new threats to privacy through the collection, storing and dissemination of personal information by computers.

Several conclusions were drawn in this study. Firstly, the increase in the handling of automated information has almost always been matched by the adoption of legislation protecting individuals from the threats posed by the computerized processing of personal data. The civil society, in particular non-governmental organizations (*inter alia*, associations of civil liberties and consumer groups) and trade unions, as well as industrialists, the liberal professions, and so on, has played its role by drawing attention to this important issue. In addition, in many countries with a federal structure, subnational data protection laws have been passed. This is a most encouraging trend.

Secondly, in countries where large-scale computerization may still be far off, there may be a need to install a regulating regime before technology expands to cover all areas of data processing. This would increase the receptivity and sensitivity to problems arising from such technology and would step up the harmonization of domestic law with the provisions of international law. In this respect, multi-disciplinary, cross-cultural research should be fostered (calling upon the juridical sciences, computer sciences, economics, information sciences, social anthropology, sociology, and the like) with a view to a wider understanding of the various aspects of data protection.

Thirdly, within the field of personal data, the area of medical data and of genetic information is receiving increasing attention from the public. Professional organizations (medical and paramedical organizations being the most prominent) and grass-roots associations have taken the initiative of adopting declarations or codes of conduct on the subject. International intergovernmental organizations have also drawn up guidelines.

In particular, genetic information has two specific features. Firstly, it concerns individuals, their families and their kin. Secondly, its relevance is partly due to its expansion in time (genetic data gathered over generations) and in space (genetic data gathered on increasingly larger populations). Collection and storing of, and access to, genetic data set crucial questions pertaining to protecting privacy and family life. How long should genetic information be kept? How can its confidential nature be ensured through time? Who has the right to reveal or to conceal such information that affects, by definition, not only an individual, but also his family and his kin? These are some of the problems that were raised by the UNESCO International Bioethics Committee, created in 1993, which will continue to work in 1994–95 on the preparation of an international instrument for the protection of the human genome.

In 1990, UNESCO requested Mr James Michael, of the Centre for Communications and Information Law, Faculty of Laws, University College, London, to examine new developments that took place in the late 1980s and to analyse the standard-setting instruments which were being prepared or had been adopted by international organizations. It should be noted that there is a growing jurisprudence, at the international level, on the protection of privacy and family life. This is particularly true of the European Commission and Court of Human Rights, based on the provisions of Article 8 of the European Convention on Human Rights.

The report is dedicated to Mr Paul Sieghart, who supervised and contributed to it before his untimely death in December 1988. His chairmanship of the Executive Committee of Justice, the British section of the International Commission of Jurists (hereafter referred to as the ICJ), and his supervision of this study on behalf of the ICJ, were only two of his many efforts to promote human rights, particularly in relation to developing technologies.

This book aims at presenting the state of the art in the area of protection of data. UNESCO thanks the author for accepting this task and hopes that the publication will increase public awareness and encourage public debate on this issue.

The ideas and opinions expressed in this book are those of the author and do not necessarily represent the views of UNESCO. In addition, the designations employed and the presentation of material throughout the publication do not imply the expression of any opinion whatsoever on the part of UNESCO concerning the legal status of any country, territory, city or area or of its authorities, or concerning its frontiers or boundaries.

Georges B. Kutukdjian
Director, Bioethics Unit
UNESCO

Introduction

The Nature and Significance of Privacy

Of all the human rights in the international catalogue, privacy is perhaps the most difficult to circumscribe and define. In its narrowest sense, some might think of it as no more than a luxury for the better-off in developed countries. At its widest, it can connote the last opportunity for the poorest and weakest human beings to defend themselves against the ever-encroaching pressures of the power groups in their societies which are forever pushing inwards the boundaries within which those unique individuals can still take final refuge, and ultimately 'be themselves'.[1]

The problem of the definition and scope of this fundamental human right has bedevilled decades of debate on the subject, and diverted all too many well-intentioned attempts to devise national legislation for its better protection. For example, the Younger Committee on Privacy in the United Kingdom decided in 1972[2] against recommending a general legal right to privacy in that country, not least because of the difficulties of defining what was to be protected.[3] (That reluctance may also have been a reflection of the general common law preference for specific remedies rather than abstract principles.)

Theoretical arguments over the definition of privacy continue unabated, as well as more practical disputes over the details of new legal rules. But the purpose of this study is not to enter either of these disputatious areas; it is rather to consider how various nations and international bodies have begun, since 1972, to further the protection of what, in the English language, is generally called 'privacy', in the light of the developments in computer technology since then; and what more remains to be done in this field.

In the international law of human rights 'privacy' is clearly and unambiguously established as a fundamental right to be protected. As early as 1948, Article 12 of the Universal Declaration of Human Rights asserted that 'no one shall be subjected to arbitrary interference with his privacy, family, home, or correspondence, nor to attacks upon his honour and reputation'. However, quite apart from

1

arguments over the definition of privacy, there are also differences of view over the categorization of privacy in the canon of human rights. Privacy is usually classified as a civil or political right, principally because it is included in the United Nations Covenant on such rights; but it could be argued that, in certain respects, it also involves questions of economic, cultural and social rights. The ICJ study of 1972 (called 'the 1972 study' hereafter) quoted Professor Alan Westin's landmark book, *Privacy and Freedom*,[4] in saying that 'privacy is at the heart of freedom in the modern state', but more recently, Professor David Flaherty has said that 'although privacy is an important instrumental value, it is not identical to such fundamental values as liberty, freedom, and democracy'.[5] It is not necessary to decide between these two emphases here, except to suggest that although privacy is important in an instrumental sense in that it is closely linked to the exercise of other rights (such as the right to receive and impart information), it also reflects a near-universal need, although one of varying content, as a fundamental value on its own.

Professor Westin's definition[6] of privacy as the desire of individuals for solitude, intimacy, anonymity, and reserve is useful, though not conclusive. So is the formulation by Dean Prosser of privacy into four 'torts'.[7] However, before proceeding to consider the impact of technology on privacy and the various legal approaches to its protection, it is perhaps appropriate to consider briefly the possible reasons and steps which lead to the placing of such a high value on it.

In considering the connotations of 'privacy', it is of some importance to recall whether one is dicussing a state or condition, a desire, a claim, or a right.[8] The state or condition is familiar enough: everyone knows what it is to be withdrawn from the society of others, to find seclusion, avoid publicity, be solitary, or retire from the world's activities. Desiring to achieve such a state or condition presents no problems by itself, but to *claim* to be entitled to achieve it at will is quite another matter; and to be given a *right* to it, even against adverse claimants, is yet another.

Perceptions of all these things differ. It is a commonplace that privacy is culture-specific: the matters which a particular society regards as 'private' can vary widely. Although anthropological evidence cannot be conclusive, it does seem that most societies regard some areas of human activity as not really suitable for general observation and knowledge. There is some evidence that even in small agricultural communities the boundaries of physical space which is 'private' are quite sharply defined, and that some kinds of personal information are also closely guarded.[9] This widespread, if not universal, desire for privacy is not limited to activities – or information about them – which would necessarily lead to unpleasant consequences, or produce guilt or shame in the person concerned.

One explanation of the human urge for privacy, advanced by Sisella Bok, is derived from anthropology and developmental psychology. The process by which an infant becomes aware of its existence as an entity apart from others seems to be connected to the realization 'that one has the power to remain silent [which is] linked to the understanding that one can exert some control over events – that one need not be entirely transparent, entirely predictable, or ... at the mercy of parents who have seemed all-seeing and all-powerful'.[10]

This explanation of the desire for privacy is closely linked with the development of the individual human personality. The Younger Committee in the UK did not linger over questions of definition, but it did assert that the need for privacy is nearly universal, and that it is not limited to human beings:

> The quest and need for privacy is a natural one, not restricted to man alone, but arising in the biological and social processes of all the higher forms of life. All animals have a need for temporary individual seclusion or the intimacy of small units, quite as much as for the stimulus of social encounters among their own species. Indeed the struggle of all animals, whether naturally gregarious or not, to achieve a balance between privacy and participation is one of the basic features of animal life.[11]

For the purposes of this study we shall therefore assume that the desire for privacy is a fundamental human characteristic which has, albeit relatively recently, been formulated as a fundamental human right – without examining further the speculative origins of its characteristics in psychological or anthropological theory.

At this point, we must draw another distinction: between privacy in all its manifold aspects, and *information* privacy as one particular aspect of it. The general claim to privacy includes such things as not to have our territory invaded by strangers, not to have our books read, or our records played, or our clothes worn, by others without our permission, even if this causes us no loss and tells those others nothing about us. But the area of 'information privacy' is narrower; here, what we claim is that others should not obtain *knowledge* about us without our consent. In Professor Westin's words, this is 'the claim of individuals, groups or institutions to determine for themselves when, how, and to what extent information about them is communicated to others'.[12] Professor Arthur Miller put it even more briefly, defining it as 'the individual's ability to control the circulation of information relating to him'.[13] This is the aspect of the general right of privacy with which the present study is principally concerned, since it is the one which has been the most profoundly affected – and some would say most dangerously threatened – by recent developments in information technology.

In that context, one fundamental question remains, and it is made more important by the development of both surreptitious surveillance devices and information-processing technology. If the choice of the individual is central to personal privacy, both in the sense of allowing physical intrusions and of sharing information, how can privacy be said to be invaded by the obtaining of information about an individual and its processing by automatic means if the individual has no knowledge that this is occurring? An easy answer lies in the 'chilling effect' doctrine first articulated by the US Supreme Court. As the West German Constitutional Court said in its 1983 decision holding a new Census Act unconstitutional:

> If someone cannot predict with sufficient certainty which information about himself in certain areas is known to his social milieu, and cannot estimate sufficiently the knowledge of parties to whom communication may possibly be made, he is crucially inhibited in his freedom to plan or decide freely and without being subject to any pressure/influence (i.e. self-determined). The right to self-determination in relation to information precludes a social order and a legal order enabling it, in which the citizens no longer can know who knows what, when and on what occasion about them. If someone is uncertain whether deviant behaviour is noted down and stored permanently as information, or is applied or passed on, he will try not to attract attention by such behaviour. If he reckons that participation in an assembly or a citizens' initiative will be registered officially and that personal risks might result from it, he may possibly renounce the exercise of his respective rights. This would not only impair his chances of development but would also impair the common good because self-determination is an elementary functional condition of a free democratic community based on its citizens' capacity to act and to cooperate.[14]

This doctrine focuses on the inhibitory effect on the exercise of other rights of knowing that one is, or may be, subject to surveillance. It is just the condition of uneasiness that was expressed in George Orwell's *1984*. As the Younger Committee reported: 'In such cases, we were told, the result would be an increase in the incidence of tension-induced mental illness or at least a decrease in the imaginativeness and creativity of the society as a whole.'[15]

Most of the writing on privacy assumes or asserts that invasions of privacy will become known to, or suspected by, those who are subject to such invasions. But a perfect system of surveillance and data processing need not even provoke suspicion. The 1972 study quoted Professor Westin's description of privacy as 'the voluntary and temporary withdrawal of a person from the general society', and said:

> Clearly, the 'withdrawal' of which A. Westin speaks is not possible when the individual is not conscious of the threat to or violation of his

privacy, in other words when information is obtained by improper means, or when, having been obtained with the knowledge of the individual, it is then used for a purpose other than that contemplated or stipulated at the time of communication.

The question is far from theoretical. In the United Kingdom it is a cardinal administrative rule of police practice (*not* one of admissibility of evidence)[16] that tapes and transcripts of intercepted telephone conversations are never used as direct evidence in court. This rule of practice is now reinforced by a statutory ban on the introduction of such evidence in nearly all criminal prosecutions.[17] Other evidence can usually be found, and if it is not, then it seems that an aquittal is an acceptable price to pay for the maintenance of secrecy. This rule of practice was explained by the British Attorney-General to the European Court of Human Rights in the *Malone* case.[18] The Court held, unanimously, that the British system of telephone-tapping by administrative warrant, and of providing the police with 'metering' information about telephone calls with no warrant of any kind, were violations of the right to privacy under Article 8 of the European Convention. As a matter of regional international law, then, such 'unperceived invasions' do violate the right to privacy, but the theoretical justification remains difficult.

Although it may not be easy to ascribe any psychological harm to an individual who is under thorough surveillance while mistakenly believing that he is not, it is possible to assert that such a system, particularly when imposed in secret by public authorities, is at the very least an unacceptable breach of the social contract between citizens and their governments which democracy entails. In this way, it is possible to explain one of the more significant developments in privacy protection law since 1972. Before that time the legal protection of privacy in most countries was, apart from constitutional statements of principle, a matter of providing legal remedies which aggrieved individuals could pursue through the courts, or at times through administrative channels. However, a central feature of data protection legislation in Europe and Canada since then has been the creation of supervisory commissions, commissioners, or boards, with the duties and powers of overseeing data users in the public and private sectors, in order to protect the privacy of what are now called data subjects. There may be a danger in such a development if it is at the expense of individual remedies, since it is always difficult to create bodies which are sufficiently independent of those to be regulated. Nevertheless, this development is essential to protect individuals from improper surveillance of which they may not be aware, as well as providing a practical solution to the question of how to resolve the difficult cases in which surveillance may be justifiable without defeating its possible purpose by disclosure to the person concerned.

The present study will therefore concentrate on the different ways in which the world's main legal systems, its international one, and countries in different categories, have sought to counter the threat of increasing data surveillance of their populations, in the light of the technological developments which have taken place since 1972.

For that purpose, we shall first outline the impact of these technological developments; briefly summarize the different approaches taken by the Nordic, civil law, and common law legal systems; and explain the principal provisions of international law on the subject. We shall then describe the relevant legislation of selected countries, in four groups: those which now have laws regulating both data protection and access to government information; those which only have data protection laws; those which only have access to government information laws; and those which, so far, have constitutional provisions but have not yet legislated in detail. Finally, we shall summarize our conclusions, and make some recommendations for further research.

The Impact of Technology on Privacy

Since the 1972 study was prepared, progress in the technologies which handle information, and therefore pose a potential threat to information privacy, has seemed quite dramatic. Yet, on closer analysis, what has in fact happened in that time is not so much that new technologies have been invented, but rather that those which were then already known have increased dramatically in their power while falling, equally dramatically, in their prices, so that they have now achieved a degree of market penetration which only their most optimistic advocates could have hoped for a decade ago. At the same time, they have converged to a high degree of mutual symbiosis.

These two connected phenomena are worth a moment's examination. Even before 1972, the more far-sighted observers had foreseen at least the possibilities of a wider spread of the techniques of electronic storage, processing, and communication of information which were then already known, but were still available only to large organizations in the public or private sectors. *Privacy and the Law*, the report of the ICJ's British section Justice which led directly to the appointment of the Younger Committee, was published in 1970.[19] Its Appendix E, entitled 'Computers and Privacy', concisely described the threat which the new technology might pose to the privacy rights of individuals, and foreshadowed the title of a White Paper to be published by the United Kingdom government on this subject five years later.[20] Martin and Norman's *The Computerised Society* was published in 1973,[21] and painted futuristic scenarios of the universal penetration of societies by the new technologies, which many then still dismissed as the mere fantasies of technocrats.

Yet, within little more than a decade, many of those fantasies have been realized. For less than a week's average industrial wage, the inhabitants of the developed world can now acquire a wide range of microcomputers capable of performing hundreds of thousands of programmed instructions per second, and storing hundreds of thousands of words of information. Perhaps even more important, they can buy for a few pounds or dollars programs which enable them to use these computers to manipulate information in highly sophisticated ways, and yet are so simple to operate that no specialized skill in computing, or anything else, is needed to use them. In the early 1970s, commentators were still grappling with the problems posed by some huge and costly 'mainframe' machines operated by highly skilled experts; today, a large proportion of all electronic data processing takes place in millions of small and increasingly portable boxes easily affordable, and usable, by a substantial proportion of a country's population.

True, the countries concerned are still predominantly those of the developed First World; but because of the tremendous market penetration of these products their prices have now fallen to such a level that, like the transistor radio in the 1960s, it cannot be long before they spread progressively through the developing world also. At the same time, the convergence of electronic data processing and telecommunications technology, already discernible in the early 1970s, has progressed at such a pace that today it is legitimate to view them both as a single technology. Increasingly, microcomputers come ready equipped to communicate with each other and with the big mainframes on which the world's very large data banks are still held, so that their users – with minimal effort, skill, and cost – can plug themselves into world-wide networks of information from which they can select what they want, and manipulate it as they please on their own machines.

It is interesting to note that in the 1972 study the polygraph was still being cited as the major threat to privacy in the area of psychological surveillance. Its use as a 'lie detector' has spread, although nothing like the use of computers, and it still remains a threat to privacy. Polygraph tests have been required in the United States for federal civil servants in efforts to trace 'leaks' of government information even if they are unrelated to national security, and there has been controversy in the United Kingdom over proposals to require polygraph tests of employees at signals intelligence installations. The use of psychological testing of employees does not quite qualify as a technological advance, although data processing may speed both the interpretation of such tests as well as the storage and retrieval of results. Nevertheless, in times of high unemployment such tests, along with tests of even less psychological validity such as graphology and compulsory medical examinations, may present a threat to the privacy of both employees and applicants. The threat of Aids and the use of drugs have led an increasing number of public and private sector employers and insurers to require medical tests and 'lifestyle' questionnaires. One danger is that employment decisions may be made on grounds that have nothing to do with genuine occupational qualifications. Another, referred to in the 1972 study as 'scientific sophism', is that employment decisions may be made on the basis of inexact information, frequently without the knowledge of the person concerned. That, at least, is one clear injustice capable of being done to individuals by invasions of their privacy without their knowledge.

That study then classified the nature of technical threats to privacy, using Professor Westin's tripartite division into physical surveillance, psychological surveillance, and data surveillance. Although there have been some advances in the first two, particularly in the use of optical and acoustical devices (which Westin had thought presented 'the greatest present threat'), it now appears that advances in data surveillance have in fact presented the greatest danger since 1972, which is doubtless why it is in that field that there has been the most concerted effort at developing juridical devices to protect privacy, through what is now commonly known as data protection legislation.

But data surveillance presupposes the collection of data in the first place. It is possible to exaggerate the threat to privacy – or at least the scale of the threat to the general population – from surveillance technology alone. In the field of visual surveillance there have been advances in light intensifiers and lightweight automatic television cameras. Although little is publicly known, it does seem clear that the use of fibre optics has made it possible for police to maintain surveillance in various hostage-taking and hijacking cases. Video recording technology makes it far easier, and less costly, to keep a record of visual surveillance than in 1972. One result of technological advances in visual and aural surveillance is that issues of invasion of privacy by surveillance become issues of 'information privacy'. It is a cliché, but nevertheless true, that the inherent inefficiency of manual filing systems was quite an effective privacy protection device until recent advances in automatic data processing. Although advances in surveillance technology may have increased the threat to the privacy of selected individuals, it is the advance in data processing to store, collate, and retrieve the results of such surveillance that presents a more general threat. The major change has been one of scale as well as intensity. For public authorities at least, it is now possible not just to know a great deal about an individual, but to 'know', in the sense of being able both to collect and retrieve information, a very great deal about almost everybody.

Telephone-tapping is a useful illustration. The introduction of electronic switching to replace semiautomatic systems (such as the Strowger one still used in parts of the United Kingdom) makes it much easier to intercept telephone conversations. The use of voice-activated tape recorders also makes automatic recording of intercepted conversations more efficient. Two technological barriers remain, however, to the use of telephone interceptions as an instrument of mass surreptitious surveillance: the effort involved in transcribing all the conversations, and the ability to retrieve particular tape-recorded conversations by reference to particular words or phrases.

Both these barriers are crumbling rapidly, however. There is already some technology for transcribing speech automatically, and searching such a transcript (or its electronic equivalent) for particular words is already feasible. The major difficulty is in developing technology to transcribe the variations of everyday speech. The ability to 'search' tape-recorded conversations may already have been achieved. Although it has not been acknowledged officially, an article in the British *New Scientist*[22] reported that international telephone conversations (and other forms of telecommunications) were already being monitored in this way.

If this is so, then what would have been considered a form of technical surveillance now also becomes a matter for data protection. Similarly, the 'metering' referred to in the *Malone* case is less a form of surveillance than a matter of constructing a 'data profile' by using information which most people would not consider to be particularly sensitive by itself. 'Metering' is recording the telephone numbers dialled from a particular telephone and the duration of the conversations, but not their contents. It is still cumbersome in much of the United Kingdom because a special meter must be attached manually at the telephone exchange. In more modern telephone systems, however, such records are printed out automatically, and are often sent to customers with their bills. Although the European Court of Human Rights held in *Malone* that providing the police with such information without some form of warrant under law was an invasion of privacy, the US Supreme Court held in 1979[23] that it was not.

Advances in telephone technology such as caller-identification and call-barring have created new threats to personal privacy while providing for privacy protection from unwanted callers. The European Community is now considering a draft directive that would attempt to resolve the competing privacy interests presented by such developments.[24] This is in conjunction with a proposal for a general Community directive on data protection and accession by the EC to the Council of Europe Convention on Data Protection.[25]

Thus, although technological advances have increased the threat to privacy from direct surveillance in some individual cases, it is modern data processing that presents the greater threat to privacy for populations in general. In one sense data processing reduces the need for surveillance by enabling the creation of 'data profiles' on individuals from publicly available information which formerly would have been difficult or impossible to retrieve and collate. The 1972 study commented that computers would make it possible 'for a person having access to the coded data on computers to bring together all the recorded information, often of a private and personal nature, about a particular person in a way that would never have been practical before'.

Two comments may now be made in enlarging upon this. The first is that it is now possible to construct a profile of a person which may be considered to be invasive of privacy from individual items of information which would *not* be considered 'private and personal'. The second, which may have been inherent in the original comment, is that the widespread use of personal computers and the existence of distributed data banks linked by public communications networks makes it possible, at least in principle, for many people to gain access to such profiles.

Notes

1 See generally, Robertson, A.H. (ed.) (1973), *Privacy and Human Rights*, Manchester: Manchester University Press.
2 Cmnd. 5092.
3 Ibid., paras. 57–73; 665.
4 Westin, A.F., *Privacy and Freedom*, p. 350, New York: Atheneum (1967); London: Bodley Head (1970).
5 Flaherty, D.H. (1984), *Privacy and Data Protection: An International Bibliography*, London: Mansell.
6 In *Privacy and Freedom, supra.*
7 Intrusion, disclosure of embarrassing private facts, presenting an individual in a 'false light', and appropriation of a name or likeness: 48 *California Law Review* 383.
8 For a discussion of these distinctions, see Sieghart, P. (1976), *Privacy and Computers*, London: Latimer.
9 See Tefft, Stanton (ed.) (1980), *Secrecy: A Crosscultural Perspective*, New York: Human Sciences Press.
10 Bok, S. (1983), *Secrets*, Oxford: Oxford University Press.
11 *Report of the Committee on Privacy* (Cmnd. 5012), para. 109.
12 *Privacy and Freedom*, p. 7.

13 Miller, A.R. (1971), *Assault on Privacy: Computers, Data Banks and Dossiers*, Ann Arbor, Mich.: University of Michigan Press, p. 40.
14 English translation in *Human Rights Law Journal*, Vol. 5, No. 1, p. 94, at 100–1.
15 Op. cit., para. 111.
16 *R.* v. *Keeton* [1970] Crim.L.R. 402.
17 Interception of Communications Act 1985.
18 Memorial of the Government of the United Kingdom in *Malone* (4/1983/60/94), Cour (83) 94 para. 2.19.
19 London: Stevens & Sons, 1970.
20 Cmnd. 6353, 1975.
21 London: Penguin Books, 1973.
22 28 February 1985, p. 6.
23 *Smith* v. *Maryland*, 442 US 735, 99 S Ct 2577 (1979).
24 Proposal for a Council Directive concerning the protection of personal data and privacy in the context of public digital telecommunications networks, in particular the integrated services digital network (ISDN) and public digital mobile networks. COM(90) 314 final -SYN 287 and 288, Brussels, 13 September 1990.
25 See Appendix 4.

1 Different Legal Approaches

Nordic Law

Although Nordic law is best known for protecting privacy through a combination of the publicity principle and specific data protection legislation, 'Nordic' is also applied to one of the better-known definitions of the right to privacy. The Nordic Conference was a meeting of legal authorities from around the world in Stockholm in 1967, organized by the International Commission of Jurists. Their declaration of what the right to privacy meant included Prosser's torts, but went beyond them. The ten relatively specific rights listed in that declaration have no legal force as such, but they are nevertheless highly persuasive, and deserve quotation here in full:

The right to privacy is the right to be left alone to live one's life with the minimum degree of interference. In expanded form, this means the right of the individual to lead his own life protected against:

1   interference with his private, family, and home life;

2   interference with his physical or mental integrity or his moral and intellectual freedom;

3   attacks on his honour and reputation;

4   being placed in a false light;

5   the disclosure of irrelevant embarrassing facts relating to his private life;

6   the use of his name, identity, or likeness;

7   spying, prying, watching and besetting;

8   interference with his correspondence;

9   disclosure of information given or received by him in circumstances of professional confidence;

10 misuse of his private communications, written or oral.

It is perhaps significant that this formulation can only be applied with some difficulty to the system of data protection that Sweden was to adopt just seven years later. Some of the rights apply to data protection more easily than others, such as 'being placed in a false light'. But the principles of data protection, as expressed in the Council of Europe Convention on the subject, demonstrate that privacy is a developing concept and that the development has been accelerated by the advance of technology.

The 1972 study began the section on Sweden by saying that 'there is very little legal protection of the privacy of the individual in Sweden and as yet only a limited demand for it'. In the area of protection of privacy from 'data surveillance', both Swedish law and public attitudes have changed radically since then. Sweden enacted the world's first national data protection law in 1973, and the British Committee on Data Protection reported[1] that a 1977 public opinion survey conducted by the Swedish National Bureau of Statistics found that privacy protection was regarded as the third most important public issue there (after unemployment and inflation). The 1972 study did report that there was growing concern in Sweden about privacy and computers, and also noted that in 1965 the Swedish Supreme Administrative Court had held that the general right of public access to government documents applied to computer-stored information. The use of this right, and the specific concern with computers, evidently pointed the direction for what may be called the Nordic approach to privacy protection.

Nordic law in general, and Swedish law in particular, has dealt with the protection of privacy through two methods: the ancient principle of governmental publicity, and the modern approach of data protection legislation. The former, called the *offentlighetsprincip*, was incorporated in the Swedish constitution in 1766, and provides a general right of public access to government documents. Although this does not seem to have been intended originally as a privacy protection measure, many of those who exercise the right do so in order to inspect records that relate to them personally. It is a form of 'subject access' to government records which provides a means of monitoring information privacy.

The Swedish *Datalagen*, or Data Protection Act, was enacted in 1973, and represents a modern approach to the privacy problems presented by data processing in both the public and the private sectors. It provides a general right of subject access to automatically processed personal data, but does not rely only, or even primarily, on that method. Instead, the Data Inspection Board acts as an administrative overseer of data processing generally, with extensive powers over all the data users who are required to register with it.

Other Scandinavian countries have generally followed Sweden in their legal approach to the protection of privacy, which is usually expressed in Swedish as *integritet*. They came much later to the adoption of the 'publicity principle', however. Finland passed an access to government information law in 1951, and has yet to adopt a data protection law. Norway legislated on access to information in 1970, and on data protection in 1978. Denmark adopted very similar legislation on the same subjects in the same years. Iceland has no access to government information law, but passed a data protection law in 1981.

The Nordic approach may be characterized as a combination of a legal remedy available to individuals through their right of access to government records, and a system of administrative regulation of computerized records. This is not to say that other methods for protecting privacy are not available in those countries. Norway has, since 1899, had a criminal statute forbidding violations of 'the peace of private life', and there has been case law which is remarkably similar to that in the USA. The Scandinavian approach to data protection legislation has greatly influenced other countries which have legislated on the subject, particularly those which are now parties to the Council of Europe's Data Protection Convention; and Jan Freese, for several years the head of Sweden's Data Inspection Board, has been a leading figure in data protection since he helped to promote the first national law in 1973.

Civil Law

The 1972 study commented, particularly regarding the protection against public disclosures about a person's private life, that there was a 'striking difference' between the protection offered by the law in the civil and the common law countries. Although perhaps less striking now, a similar comment could be made about the generally different approaches to privacy in the two legal traditions. Although there are specific remedies for particular invasions of privacy in France and other civil law countries, the notion of privacy can be traced back there to a provision in the Declaration of the Rights of Man and the Citizen of 1789 declaring private property to be inviolable and sacred. The history of privacy protection law in the United Kingdom begins much earlier, with the provision of the Justices of the Peace Act 1361 enabling eavesdroppers and 'Peeping Toms' to be bound over to keep the peace; continues through judicial decisions in such cases as *Entick* v. *Carrington*[2] and *Prince Albert* v. *Strange*,[3] and remains resolutely particular.

The civil law approach, with its emphasis on statements of general principle, has had a clear influence on two significant institutions in the development of privacy law: the Constitution of the United States and the codification of international human rights law, particularly in the substance and procedures of the European Convention on Human Rights. Both these instruments owe much to the civil law for assertions of principle, but both also owe much to the common law method of applying such principles through case law (or jurisprudence). The combination of a written constitution with the doctrine of binding precedent enabled the US Supreme Court to 'find' a constitutional right to privacy in *Griswold* v. *Connecticut*.[4] The right of individual petition to the European Commission of Human Rights under Article 25 of the Convention has enabled the Commission and the Court to develop the right to privacy under the Convention in cases such as *Klass*[5] and *Malone*.[6]

The traditions of the civil law also include the establishment of invigilatory institutions to prevent harm before it occurs – a solution adopted, in the context of data protection, initially in the Nordic countries, and since then elsewhere, including the common law jurisdictions of the United Kingdom and Canada.

Common Law

The common law approach in the United Kingdom (or, more precisely, in England, Wales, and Northern Ireland) is one of particular legal remedies against particular infringements, and the rights are often developed by judges without the assistance of Parliament. To take a leading example from privacy law, the essentials of the law of confidence described in the well-known case of *Prince Albert* v. *Strange*[7] had been asserted by judges in earlier cases, and the doctrine has yet to be restated by Parliament in any way (although the Law Commission has proposed that it be reformed and put into statutory form, and the government has indicated that it is now contemplating the introduction of such a statute).[8] The fact that there is no general legal right to privacy in the domestic law of the United Kingdom does not mean that there is no legal protection for privacy. Similarly, the fact that the US Supreme Court has declared that there is a general constitutional right to privacy does not mean that privacy is always better protected in the USA than in the United Kingdom. The ability of a 'public figure' in the USA to protect his or her reputation using the law of defamation is considerably less under the Supreme Court decision in *New York Times* v. *Sullivan*[9] than in the United Kingdom (although some think this justifiable because of the competing interest in freedom of the press).

The common law of privacy developed far more quickly in the United States than in the United Kingdom following *Prince Albert's* case (which, strictly speaking, was a case in equity rather than at common law). There were three strands to this development: the creation of new torts of invasions of privacy, the development of a constitutional doctrine, and the introduction of specific legislative measures at the state and federal level. It is unlikely that the Supreme Court would have declared a constitutional right to privacy if there had not been a prior growth of judge-made and statutory rights.

In the United Kingdom the law of breach of confidence was largely used to protect commercially valuable information until the case of *Argyll* v. *Argyll*,[10] when it was applied to prevent an ex-spouse from disclosing marital secrets. Since then it has been applied in various novel ways, occasionally to protect personal privacy but also to protect commercial and governmental information.[11] Although the common law approach in both the United Kingdom and the USA still tends to favour specific remedies for particular invasions of privacy, those remedies are increasingly statutory rather than judge-made. As has perhaps been suggested in the comments on Nordic and civil law, international trends in data protection and access to government information legislation have resulted in similar institutions. Although the Council of Europe's Data Protection Convention does not expressly require the establishment of a national data protection authority, most countries which have signed the Convention have adopted such a mechanism.

Thus the United Kingdom, the home of common law, has adopted legislation establishing a Data Protection Registrar, with powers and responsibilities remarkably like those of the CNIL in France. The contribution of common law to the protection of privacy was, for a long time, the fertile development of specific rights by US judges. That development is still useful, but civil law institutions have been more prominent recently, particularly in the field of data protection. There is no single ideal legal method of protecting the complex of values under the privacy label, and, with careful adjustments and nurturing, institutions can be transplanted from one legal tradition to another. The spread of the Nordic institution of the ombudsman is one example, and data protection seems likely to be another. The easy transfer of information across frontiers makes it particularly important not only that privacy protection should not be confined to particular countries and legal traditions, but that common international standards should be established, with effective mechanisms for their enforcement. That is the subject of the next chapter.

Notes

1　Cmnd. 7341, para. 4.05 (1978).
2　(1765) 19 State Trials 1029.
3　(1849) 1 Mac. & G. 25.
4　381 US 479 (1965).
5　*Klass* v. *Federal Republic of Germany*, judgment of 6 September 1978, Series A, No. 28.
6　*Malone* v. *United Kingdom*, judgment of 2 August 1984, No. 4/1983/60/94.
7　(1849) 1 Mac. & G. 25.
8　Statement to Parliament of Mr Leon Brittan, Home Secretary; *Hansard*, 12 March 1985, col. 157.
9　376 US 254 (1964).
10　[1967] Ch. 302.
11　As in the unsuccessful attempt to stop publication of a cabinet minister's diaries in *Attorney-General* v. *Jonathan Cape* [1976] QB 752.

2 International Standards

International Human Rights Instruments

*The Universal Declaration and the International Covenant on Civil and
Political Rights*

International statements of the right to privacy, like all such international formulations, are necessarily cast in general terms. But the right
to privacy articulated in Article 12 of the Universal Declaration of
Human Rights 1948 included some quite specific provisions in saying that: 'No one shall be subjected to arbitrary interference with his
privacy, family, home or correspondence, nor to attacks upon his
honour and reputation. Everyone has the right to the protection of
the law against such interference or attacks.' Already the concept of
individual privacy has thus been extended to include the kinship
'zone' of the family.[1] The physical zone of protection includes the
home, and correspondence with others, which may go very far from
the physical home.

The main objective of the Covenant was to reinforce the Universal
Declaration by specific treaty law. There is as yet little material interpreting the right to privacy guaranteed by Article 17 of the International Covenant on Civil and Political Rights which approaches the
jurisprudence interpreting the corresponding guarantee in Article 8
of the European Convention on Human Rights. But reports of the
drafting process and commentaries on it give some idea of what
specific rights were intended to be protected.

The words of Article 17 are identical to those used in the Universal
Declaration. The right there declared, however, is closely associated
with several other rights, both in that Covenant and in the Covenant
on Economic, Social and Cultural Rights. Some of these are the
freedoms of thought, conscience, and religion; the right to determine
the moral and religious education of one's children; and the right of
association and non-association. Taking note of such an overlap, one

writer was moved to comment that: 'Indeed, in one sense all human rights are aspects of the right of privacy.'[2]

During the preparatory work for the Covenant, there seems to have been some debate over the words 'arbitrary or unlawful', and the United Kingdom found 'arbitrary' particularly unsatisfactory.[3] Although the debate is not completely over, it seems that the use of both words is not redundant, but has two implications. One is that 'arbitrariness' may include invasions of privacy which are committed within the law, particularly when an abuse of administrative discretion is involved. The other is that 'unlawful' includes invasions of privacy by entities other than government, and imposes an obligation on states to provide laws to protect their inhabitants against such invasions. There were proposals to include a limitation clause describing acceptable limits to the right to privacy, but this was rejected (unlike the approach taken in drafting Article 8 of the European Convention on Human Rights). It is in commentaries on the right that more specific examples are given. In addition to the ten definitions of the Nordic Conference already mentioned above, the Conference listed eleven more specific illustrations. These included invasions expressed in general terms, such as 'public exposure of private matters', and more specific invasions such as 'harassment of a person (for example, by observation or bothersome telephone calls)'.[4] Another writer has produced a more comprehensive list of activities and situations suggested by the principles, including 'facts relating to one's own body which are held to be repugnant or socially unacceptable' and 'in general, any personal data, fact or activity which is unknown to others, the general knowledge of which would produce moral or physical discomfort to the subject (such as nudity, premarital pregnancy)'.[5]

The debate over methods of implementing the protection of human rights in international law extends far beyond the subject of the present study. It is relevant, however, to comment that regional procedures which allow the development of case law through individual petitions at least provide concrete examples of where claims for privacy prevail over other claims. The Human Rights Committee's examinations of national reports referred to it under Article 40 have, however, given some indication of the areas of concern under Article 17. Questions have been asked, for example, about measures to protect individual privacy from automated information systems, and about safeguards to protect privacy from national intelligence services.[6]

It is not clear why the family and the home were included in the Declaration and the Covenant, and the family is provided with a degree of protection by Article 23(1). The inclusion of 'honour and reputation' did provoke some discussion, and one account of the

Third Committee's deliberations suggested a distinction between the two. The conclusion was that personal integrity is based on subjective (honour) as well as objective (reputation) elements.[7]

Some light on the meaning of the right to privacy in the UN Declaration and the Covenant is also cast by some other international instruments. For example, secrecy of correspondence is guaranteed by Article 22 of the International Telecommunication Convention, albeit with qualifications:

> Members agree to take all possible measures, compatible with the system of telecommunication used, with a view to ensuring the secrecy of international correspondence. Nevertheless, they reserve the right to communicate such correspondence to the competent authorities in order to ensure the application of their internal laws or the execution of international conventions to which they are parties.

Some General Assembly resolutions have particular application to the effects of technology on the right to privacy. The 1968 Resolution,[8] taking note of the Teheran Proclamation, invited the Secretary-General to undertake a study of human rights problems arising from developments in science and technology, in particular, 'Respect for the privacy of individuals ... in the light of advances in recording and other techniques; and uses of electronics which may affect the rights of the person and the limits which should be placed on such uses in a democratic society.' Declaration 3348 in 1975 was more specific, calling on states to take measures to protect all strata of the population from the harmful effects of the misuse of scientific and technological developments, 'including their misuse to infringe upon the rights of the individual or of the group, particularly with regard to respect for privacy and the protection of the human personality and its physical and intellectual integrity'.

In 1976 a report by the Secretary-General included several specific points 'for possible inclusion in draft international standards concerning respect for the privacy of the individual in the light of modern recording and other devices'.[9] Not all of its proposals are limited to privacy and technology, such as licensing of private detectives and establishment of journalists' codes of ethics. It has not yet found expression in international law, but the specific character of its recommendations make it worth quoting in full:

> 177.   In view of the considerable differences of opinion as to the practical effects which the creation on the national level of a statutory right to privacy would have on the protection of other rights, as well as of the different legal contexts in which such legislation would operate, it seems inadvisable to recommend a uniform adoption of legislation establishing a general right to privacy. International standards

might, however, be adopted, indicating other types of action which should be taken to protect the privacy of the individual against invasions by modern recording and other techniques, along the following lines:

1.   States shall adopt legislation, or bring up to date existing legislation, so as to provide protection for the privacy of the individual against invasions by modern technological devices;

2.   Legislation might be drafted in such a manner as to make it easily adaptable to future technological developments;

3.   States shall, in particular, take the following minimum steps:

(a) Penal Codes should designate as offences and provide for penalties of fine, imprisonment, or both, for:

i. the clandestine monitoring or recording of conversations except, possibly, by participants to the conversations, and except by judicial or ministerial order, and in accordance with that order, in countries which permit monitoring or recording in criminal investigation or for reasons of national security;

ii. the disclosure by any person of information so obtained;

iii. the clandestine viewing, photographing, filming or televising of members of households and their guests in their dwellings, except by judicial or ministerial order, and in accordance with that order, in countries which permit such actions in criminal investigations or for reasons of national security;

(b) States which permit the utilization by their own agencies of modern recording and other techniques in the investigation of crimes or for reasons of national security shall make provision to restrict the use of these techniques to cases of the most serious crimes or the most serious threats to national security. They shall lay down by law the conditions for their use, which conditions shall include:

i. prior authorization in each case by a judicial authority (or by an official of Ministerial rank), upon a showing of 'probable cause' or its equivalent and a showing that alternative methods of surveillance are not available or not effective in the particular case;

ii. specification, in the authorization, of the person to be monitored, the suspected offence, the person who is to do the monitoring, and the length of the period of surveillance. States shall make provision to ensure that such authorizations are not issued in a routine manner or by delegation of authority;

iii. specification of the extent to which use may be made in criminal proceedings of information gained;

(c) States permitting the operations of private detectives shall license such detectives individually;

(d) States shall favour the establishment of journalists' codes of ethics including provisions concerning respect for the privacy of the individual;

(e) In addition to any possible criminal liability, civil liability should attach to either the use of an auditory or visual device in relation to a person, under circumstances which would entitle him to assume that he could not be seen or heard by unauthorized persons, or the un-authorized disclosure of information so gained;

(*f*) Civil remedies shall allow a person to apply for the cessation of acts thus violating his privacy and, where the act has been completed, to recover damages, including damages for non-pecuniary injury;

(*g*) Legislative or administrative steps shall be taken to control effec-tively the importation, manufacture, advertisement, sale, transfer and possession of devices suitable primarily for clandestine auditory or visual surveillance. These steps shall include the following:

i. the manufacturers of such devices shall be required to hold a valid government licence, renewable periodically and revocable for good cause, and to submit appropriate records periodically for State inspection;

ii. the manufacturers of such devices shall be forbidden to sell them to anyone not having a valid government licence authorizing possession thereof;

iii. the unlicensed manufacture or possession of such devices shall be punishable;

iv. the responsible governmental authority shall compile and keep current a catalogue of the devices and components subject to its control;

(*h*) Legal provision shall be made for the confiscation and destruction without compensation of recording and other devices utilized in an offence involving clandestine auditory or visual surveillance, whether or not the device was intended primarily for such use.

4. States shall establish expert bodies to follow scientific and techno-logical developments affecting the right to privacy and to draw the attention of the legislature, the executive and the public to the effects of such developments, existing or new, upon the right to privacy and to possible safeguards required.

This is, at the very least, useful for any national legislature consid-ering some forms of privacy protection. From a British perspective, some of the points, such as the regulation of surveillance devices, resemble recommendations of the Younger Committee Report in 1972.[10] (The Committee was not permitted to consider possible inva-sions of privacy by government.) Others, such as those on intercep-tions of communications, are beginning to emerge from the case law of the European Convention. The Secretary-General's report was clearly directed at the effect on personal privacy of technology through surveillance by device. Several countries have already legislated on this subject, most of them by making acts criminal rather than by licensing devices. Those that have regulated devices have often done so by creating offences of unauthorised broadcasting, as many listen-ing devices require radio transmissions, usually over short distances. But these points have not yet been taken up in any enforceable re-gional convention.

That is not the case, however, with the companion report[11] of the same year, 'Points for Possible Inclusion in Draft International Standards for the Protection of the Rights of the Individual against Threats Arising from the Use of Computerized Personal Data Systems'. That report is, in international law, the parent of both the Council of Europe Data Protection Convention and the OECD Guidelines on the same subject (although both organizations had begun consideration of the problems before 1976). Although even more detailed than the points on surveillance, it also deserves full quotation. It is perhaps some indication of the urgency which was felt that only nine years, a short time in international legislation, elapsed between the publication of the UN data protection points and the coming into effect of the Council of Europe's Convention.

320. In the light of the existing and proposed safeguards dealt with in this present report, it is suggested that the following points be taken into account in the drafting of international standards relating to the protection of the rights of the individual against threats arising from the use of computerized personal data systems:

i. The States which have not yet done so should adopt appropriate legislation containing rules relating to computerized personal data systems in both the public and private sectors. As far as possible, legislation should be adopted concerning all types of computerized personal data systems (statistical and research systems, administrative systems, and intelligence systems), but may vary according to the nature of those types of systems.

ii. The following minimum standards should be followed in drawing up national legislation:
   (*a*) only the personal information strictly necesary for the purposes of the respective system should be collected;
   (*b*) the individual should be notified that information is being gathered about him and his agreement should be obtained before the information is stored, provided that information may be gathered without such knowledge and agreement in areas related to national security, law enforcement and criminal justice, and in other areas for which the law has established that such knowledge and agreement are not required due to the purpose of the gathering of information, subject to appropriate safeguards for human rights which should include those suggested in points 3(*a*)(i) and (iii) and 3(*b*) appearing in paragraph 177 of document E/CN. 4/1116;
   (*c*) the collection and storage of hearsay and other subjective material should be avoided;
   (*d*) data concerning political and religious views, race and ethnic origin and intimate life should not be collected and stored, except under conditions explicitly provided by the law;
   (*e*) all necessary measures, including technical procedures, should be taken to maintain the accuracy, completeness and pertinence of

the stored information, and to remove or update obsolete information;

(*f*) legal responsibility should rest upon computer manufacturers and/or software developers, who with knowledge or through gross negligence fail to install basic safeguards for confidentiality and security of information;

(*g*) the individual should have the right, through special procedures laid down by the law, to receive a copy, intelligible to him, of stored information relating to him, to challenge it, to add explanations to it, and to obtain the correction or removal of inaccurate, obsolete or unverifiable data about him;

(*h*) the stored information should be disclosed or otherwise used only for the purposes for which it has been collected and disclosed only to legally authorized authorities or persons;

(*i*) all necessary measures, including technical procedures, to protect the confidentiality of the data and prevent their unauthorized disclosure and dissemination should be taken;

(*j*) any damage suffered by the individual in his rights, by the misuse of computerized data concerning him, should be compensated;

(*k*) violations of laws aiming at protecting the rights of the person to whom the stored information relates should be made punishable;

(*l*) the legality of decisions about individuals based on computerized personal data systems and their judicial control should be ensured.

iii. The use as evidence of information stored in computerized systems should be regulated by special legislation.

iv. Rules should protect the rights of the person whenever information about him is stored in computerized systems operating in countries other than his own.

v. The establishment of a supervisory body in the field of operation of computerized personal data systems should be considered. Its functions might include:

(*a*) registering existing computerized personal data systems;

(*b*) supervising the observance of existing laws protecting human rights against the abuse of such systems;

(*c*) following developments in the field affecting human rights and drawing the attention of the legislature, the executive and the public to the effects of such developments upon human rights and to possible further required safeguards.

vi. The establishment of professional associations for computer personnel should be promoted and such associations should be encouraged to adopt codes of ethics which should contain minimum rules aiming at regulating the professional conduct of such personnel in such a manner as to prevent infringements of human rights.

vii. Professional associations for computer personnel might be given some jurisdiction over the professional education and the selection of such personnel and the power to apply disciplinary measures for non-compliance with the code of ethics mentioned above.

In 1990 a set of draft Guidelines for the regulation of computerized personal data files was submitted to the United Nations General Assembly. They were adopted by the General Assembly on 14 December 1990 by Resolution 45/95. The Guidelines are to be found in Appendix C of this book. These Guidelines state the following principles as minimum guarantees to be incorporated into national legislation:

1. Lawfulness and fairness;
2. Accuracy;
3. Specification of the purpose of the file;
4. Access by the concerned individual;
5. Non-discrimination;
6. Authority that can decide on exceptions;
7. Protection of files from destruction and misuse;
8. Supervision and sanctions;
9. Transborder data flows.

In addition, this standard-setting instrument specifies its field of application and makes provisions concerning personal data files kept by governmental and non-governmental international organizations.

We shall now comment very briefly on the American Declaration of the Rights and Duties of Man and the American Convention on Human Rights before reviewing in more detail the European Convention on Human Rights.

The American Declaration of the Rights and Duties of Man, and the American Convention on Human Rights

Article V of the American Declaration of 1948 says that 'Every person has the right to the protection of the law against abusive attacks upon his honor, his reputation, and his private and family life.' This is a regional declaration, and has been reinforced by the American Convention on Human Rights of 1969. Article 11 of this Convention is similar, but not identical, to the words of the UN Declaration and the Covenant:

1. Everyone has the right to have his honor respected and his dignity recognized.
2. No one may be the subject of arbitrary or abusive interference with his private life, his family, his home, or his correspondence, or of unlawful attacks on his honor or reputation.
3. Everyone has the right to protection of the law against such interference or attacks.

These provisions have not yet been applied or interpreted in the way that their older equivalents in the European Convention on Human Rights have been.

The European Convention on Human Rights

Article 8 of the European Convention differs substantially in its formulation of the right of privacy as declared in the Universal Declaration and the Covenant, both as to content and as to method of interpretation. As in many of the Convention rights, it is formulated in two paragraphs. The first is a statement of the right very like that of the Declaration and the Covenant:

> (1) Everyone has the right to respect for his private and family life, his home and his correspondence.

The second sets out the qualifications:

> (2) There shall be no interference by a public authority with the exercise of this right except such as is in accordance with the law and is necessary in a democratic society in the interests of national security, public safety or the economic well-being of the country, for the prevention of disorder or crime, for the protection of health or morals, or for the protection of the rights and freedoms of others.

The Commission and Court have rarely attempted a precise definition of 'private life' or the reasons for the provision, but in one case the Commission used language similar to that of the German Constitution's provisions, in its Article 2(1), for the 'free determination of personality'. A Belgian hotel-keeper had complained that the law which prohibited him from keeping alcohol in his home which was adjacent to the hotel violated his right to privacy. The Commission found that it was an interference with his privacy but that it was justified under the second paragraph of the Article. As to privacy, the Commission said:

> The scope of the right to respect for private life is such that it secures to the individual a sphere within which he can freely pursue the development of his personality. In principle, whenever the state enacts rules for the behaviour of the individual within this sphere, it interferes with the respect for private life.[12]

However, the Commission has also decided that the development of personality does not include the right to have a dog when this is prohibited by a local ordinance.[13]

The Commission and the Court take the elements of the Article in turn. The first question is whether the facts complained of present any question of the rights in the first sentence at all. If so, the next question is whether the facts present any 'interference' with the right. If that is established, then two basic questions are presented by the second paragraph of Article 8: was the interference in accordance with the law, and are the aims of the interference permissible and proportional for one of the interests described? The rights in Article 8 are subject to derogation in time of war and public emergency under Article 15, as well as permissible reservations under Article 64. If a country has no law protecting particular aspects of privacy, then there may be a violation of Article 13 as well.

The acceptance of the right of individual petition has been very nearly the sole source of the case law interpreting Article 8.[14] Much of this has been concerned with prisoners' rights and family life, sometimes combining the two. Although the subject of prisoners' rights involves issues beyond the scope of this study, it is particularly relevant to privacy because the very act of imprisonment removes one layer of privacy by subjecting the prisoner to a degree of surveillance. It is also relevant because at least one purpose of imprisonment is to 'reform' the prisoner. This often involves precisely the sort of invasive behaviour that is intended to change a personality, or to replace unacceptable patterns of behaviour with acceptable ones. Jeremy Bentham's Panopticon was a prison design to allow constant visual surveillance (auditory surveillance was abandoned because it would have functioned both ways in the eighteenth century). Although never actually built by him, the Panopticon inspired much of nineteenth century prison design, and is used as a potent metaphor in Foucault's *Discipline and Punish*.

In the relatively early 'confidence-building' period, the Commission (which filters complaints and attempts a 'friendly solution' before reporting on them or referring them further) tended to accept interferences with the privacy of prisoners as 'inherent' in imprisonment.[15] Now, however, the Commission follows the approach outlined above. The tendency is to find that the activity complained of is an interference with the prisoner's private life, but that it is justified by reasons such as the prevention of disorder or crime, the interests of public safety, or the protection of the rights and freedoms of others. Examples of such justifiable invasions of privacy include intimate body searches and the denial of conjugal relations.[16]

Some of the most important cases involving interference with correspondence have involved prisoners. Initially, there was a tendency to uphold interferences with prisoners' correspondence as inherent in imprisonment.[17] Now, however, largely as a result of two major decisions by the Court, both concerning the United Kingdom, interferences with the right of prisoners to correspond with the outside world must be specifically justified under paragraph 2 of Article 8.

Golder was the first of these, in which the Court found an unjustifiable interference in the Home Secretary's refusal to permit a prisoner to write to a solicitor to seek legal advice.[18] *Silver* was less condemnatory, but at least required some form of discernable administrative rules about censorship of prisoners' post.[19]

The requirement that interferences with correspondence must be both provided for by law and justifiable for one of the reasons specified in the Article has also been considered in cases involving telephone-tapping. The 1972 study included country reports on both Germany and the United Kingdom about their legal regulation of telephone-tapping. Both have now been considered by the Court: Germany's system was found to be in compliance with the Convention; the United Kingdom's was not. In *Klass*[20] the Court considered complaints that the German system of intercepting telephone communications was an unjustifiable interference with privacy. One seemingly minor point in the judgment is important in considering the justiciability of what may be called 'unperceived, but suspected' violations of privacy: although the applicants did not have clear proof that their conversations had been intercepted, they were entitled to claim the status of 'victims' of the system of interference. The German system of authorization for interceptions in the interests of national security involved scrutiny by a parliamentary panel, and relatively short time periods for authorizations.

In contrast, the British system was unanimously held by the Court to violate Article 8. The 1972 study noted that there was no judicial control of telephone-tapping in the United Kingdom, but commented that there was 'unusually strict administrative control of authorized interceptions and there is no reason to believe that this practice is carried out to any greater extent than in other countries'.[21] The British Attorney-General's description of the system of administrative control did not persuade the Court that it met the basic requirement of Article 8 that interferences must be provided for *by law* before their justification on one of the enumerated grounds could be considered. As mentioned earlier, the Court held that the system of providing the police with 'metering' information about telephone numbers dialled was also an interference which violated Article 8. In this particular ruling, the Court went beyond the case law of the US Supreme Court, which has provided privacy theorists with many particular illustrations of where the assertion of a general right to privacy can lead.[22]

Other claims that government surveillance violates the right to privacy under the Convention have been less successful. In one case the applicant had taken part in a non-violent but disruptive demonstration against the South African government during a rugby match. She was arrested and photographed during the demonstration and again at the police station, where she was told that her photograph would be kept so that if she caused trouble at future matches she could be identified and charged. The Commission found that there was no interference with her private life because her home had not been entered, that the photographs were of a public incident in which she participated voluntarily, and that there was no indication that the photographs would be made public or used for any other purpose than identification in the future.[23] It is not entirely clear whether the case means that photographing someone in public without his consent is itself not an interference with his privacy, or whether it was the further circumstances of a public demonstration followed by the limited use of photographs by the police which made it not an interference. In a much earlier case the Commission had found that police photography which was not connected with a public event was an interference with privacy, but that it was justified.[24]

Those applications involved surveillance which was known to the subjects at the time. There seems to be only one case in which 'unperceived' surveillance was involved (apart from the telephone-tapping in *Klass*). The applicant was an Austrian communist who was charged, at the request of a neo-fascist organization, with wilful bodily harm and destruction of property during a demonstration. He was acquitted, but learned during the trial that a report on him had been submitted to the court by the Vienna Federal Police Directorate. The report included the information that he had participated in political children's holiday camps in 1961, 1963, and 1972, when he was seven, nine, and eighteen years old, and that he had been responsible for publication of a student communist newspaper. None of these activities violated any law, and he had no criminal convictions. The Commission found that the use of such information in criminal proceedings was clearly necessary for the prevention of crime.[25] It is not clear whether the actual surveillance which produced the information involved an interference with privacy, although the Commission found no evidence that the applicant had been individually subjected to secret surveillance (the federal police had said that they had collected the information from records kept in accordance with laws on registration with the police and press law).

The question of whether this sort of 'data surveillance' interferes with privacy came before the Court in the case of *Leander* v. *Sweden*,[26] in which a carpenter was refused work at a naval museum on security grounds. The Court ruled that the invasion of his privacy was justified in the interests of national security, and that the Article 10 right to receive and impart information did not include an affirmative right of access to government records. The Court said that Article 10 only 'prohibits a Government from restricting a person from receiving information that others may wish or may be willing to impart to him'. The Court repeated in *Gaskin* v. *United Kingdom*[27] that Article 10 does not include an affirmative right of access to government information, but found that his Article 8 right to privacy did give him a right to certain kinds of information about his childhood in the care of public authorities.

In the case of an application challenging the British census as a violation of Article 8 the Commission found in favour of the United Kingdom.[28] The Commission considered that the census was a *prima facie* interference with the right to privacy, but that it was in accordance with the law and necessary for the economic well-being of the country. In so concluding, the Commission was particularly influenced by assurances that census returns were treated in complete confidence, that names and addresses were not to be included in the computer processing, and that the forms would not be passed to the Public Record Office for 100 years.

The European Commission and Court of Human Rights have now produced a considerable body of reasoned interpretations of the right to privacy in particular instances. They have changed interpretations over time concerning some of the more difficult questions, particularly those involving sex and the family. In *Van Oosterwijck* v. *Belgium*, for example, the Commission considered a complaint by a transsexual who argued that his government's failure to allow a civil change in sexual status to reflect a physical change (he had been born female, but had acquired male appearance through surgery) was a fundamental failure to respect private life.[29] The Commission seemed sympathetic, but the Court later rejected the claims of transsexuals to changed birth certificates in *Rees* and *Cossey* v. *United Kingdom*.

In considering national laws regulating sexual behaviour the Commission and Court have fairly consistently considered that such laws interfere with privacy, and then considered whether the interference was a justifiable one. The Court has held that a law which prohibits all homosexual relations in private between consenting male adults over the age of 21 violates Article 8,[30] because this is not 'necessary' in a 'democratic society' even if it reflects the views of the majority in that society. However, there seems to be a balancing of interests to protect children and adolescents which allows a greater margin of appreciation for the regulation of homosexual than of heterosexual activity. The Commission has found that protecting the rights and freedoms of others justifies laws making homosexual activity criminal at an age (18) at which heterosexual activity would be legal.[31]

In one case the Commission considered a claim that the right to privacy was interfered with by laws restricting abortion; it was very like the US case of *Roe* v. *Wade*[32] in balancing the privacy claim of a pregnant woman against the interests of the developing foetus. The Commission's findings differed from those of the US Supreme Court, however.[33] Upon becoming pregnant, they said, the woman's private life became connected with that of the foetus, and her claim that her right to privacy included a right to an abortion failed.

The case law under the Convention regarding family life is not limited to claims under Article 8. Article 12 separately guarantees the right to marry and found a family, and Article 2 of the First Protocol provides the right of parents to ensure that their children's education conforms to their own religious and philosophical convictions. The Commission and the Court have concentrated on biological and social families, and have refused to distinguish between legitimate and illegitimate children and their parents.[34]

International Data Protection Law

In international circles, concern about the potential effect of automatic data processing upon the right to privacy began to grow during the late 1960s and early 1970s. But the eventual drafting of international measures specifically for the purpose of protecting privacy interests against the possible misuse of information by automatic means was carried out entirely by regional institutions, mostly European ones. Although the relatively rapid growth of this activity in data protection was deliberately directed at protecting one aspect of personal privacy, it is very unlikely that it would have grown so rapidly had it not been for a quite unexpected economic aspect. Some countries, especially those committed by treaty to reducing tariff barriers, began to fear that others might use their national data protection laws as non-tariff trade barriers. The development of international standards would not only establish minimum requirements for national legislation, but it could also be used to create a community of countries which met those requirements and which agreed on a free market of information among themselves, to the potential exclusion of others.

These efforts were made largely by three co-operating institutions: the Council of Europe, the Organisation for Economic Co-operation and Development (OECD), and the European Economic Community (EEC). Of the three, the Council of Europe took the lead in developing a legal instrument. This may have been because the Council already had responsibility for development of the right to privacy guaranteed by Article 8 of the European Convention on Human Rights. The Parliamentary Assembly of the Council adopted a recommendation[35] in 1968 for an examination of the domestic law of member states and of the Convention to consider whether the right to privacy was adequately protected against developments in technology.

The OECD formed a Computer Utilization Group in 1969, which in turn created a Data Bank Panel in 1970. The Panel produced a series of reports on data protection and transborder data flow, and in 1973 was asked by the French government to consider international steps towards a harmonization of standards for national data protection laws.

Meanwhile, the Council of Europe continued with the formation, by its Legal Affairs Committee, of the Committee of Experts on Privacy and Computers in 1971. They proposed international legislation, and prepared two resolutions: one for the private sector, and another for the public sector. The first was adopted by the Committee of Ministers in 1973, and the second in 1974.[36] The 1973 resolution included words that were to lead to a later divergence between data protection laws over the protection given to legal as well as natural persons:

> In accordance with general principles of law, the notion of 'persons' used in the Resolution includes both individuals and legal persons. Legal persons have the same rights as physical persons, save those rights which are applicable only to the latter. The Committee recalled that this is also one of the underlying principles of the European Convention on Human Rights. In many cases individuals realize their rights through the intermediary body having legal personality.

The Legal Affairs Committee of the Council of Europe began to consider implementation of these resolutions by the possible preparation of a draft convention, and in 1976 a new Committee of Experts on Data Protection was formed and instructed 'to prepare a convention for the protection of privacy in relation to data processing abroad and transfrontier data processing'. The first meeting of this Committee resulted in an exchange of letters between the Council of Europe and the OECD, agreeing on mutual assistance and co-operation. Dr Frits Hondius, then of the Council of Europe's Legal Affairs Directorate, made three alternative proposals, including the one eventually adopted (with a modification), for a convention that could be ratified by countries outside Europe. A draft convention was produced by the Committee of Experts in May 1979, and a final version in April 1980.

The European Economic Community first considered data protection in a 1973 report, which was followed by debates in the European Parliament in 1974 and 1975. Thereafter, work continued within the committees of the Parliament and under the Commission. The Parliamentary Legal Affairs Committee established a subcommittee on data processing and individual rights in 1976. The Directorate-General for Industrial and Technological Affairs also established a Group of Experts on Data Processing and Privacy in 1976. They decided to wait for the Council of Europe's draft convention before proceeding with any Community legislation such as a draft directive. The Parliamentary subcommittee reported in April 1979 (just a month before the Council of Europe draft convention was published). Their resolution was endorsed by the Legal Affairs Committee, then referred to the Parliament, and adopted in June 1979. Along with the privacy elements appropriate to a resolution entitled 'On the Protection of the Rights of the Individual in the Face of Technical Developments in Data Processing', the resolution stressed the creation of a genuine common market in data processing, and pointed out that national provisions to protect privacy have a direct influence on such a common market, and, 'in particular, distort the conditions of competition'.

The OECD continued to co-operate with the Council of Europe through the Data Bank Panel, and held major international seminars such as that on Transborder Data Flows and the Protection of Privacy in Vienna in 1977. One result was the creation of a new Expert Group on Transborder Data Barriers and Protection of Privacy in 1978 to draft guidelines for the OECD in consultation with their Council of Europe and EEC counterparts. These guidelines were approved in 1979. In the Parliamentary Assembly of the Council of Europe, where European developments more or less began with the 1968 recommendation, another recommendation was adopted in 1980. This[37] recommended that the Committee of Ministers consider the possibility that a right to data protection be added to the European Convention on Human Rights.

At this point it may be useful to consider some points of view which had emerged from all these discussions. It may also be appropriate to consider how hypothetical the use of national data protection laws as non-tariff barriers was, and is.

There were, and are, some participants in this continuing round of meetings who consider the whole effort as a part of the international human rights movement, and particularly as a measure to protect the privacy of natural persons. They sometimes have frank exchanges of views with those who see privacy as a limited and dated concept, and who argue that modern information-driven societies need a comprehensive set of rules about the flow of information in general, and that the rules will be distorted if they concentrate on information concerning natural persons only.[38] There are, of course, many positions between these two, including those who consider data protection to be a complementary measure to legislation which attempts to make public administration more transparent. There are also some who see the issues almost entirely in terms of international economics. The Council of Europe's Convention and the OECD Guidelines are designed to encourage the open flow of information by harmonizing national data protection laws, just as other conventions encourage harmonization of other aspects of informatics such as technical standards.

The possibility that national data protection laws might impede transborder data flows is certainly real, and perhaps it has happened more than has been reported, just as it is said that there is more computer crime than is reported. But when the United Kingdom's Lindop Committee reported in 1978, they gave two examples in which the Swedish data protection authorities had refused permission for the export of personal data to the United Kingdom for processing, because of the absence of British data protection legislation.[39] One case involved the production of plastic health care cards, the other the printing of a register of Swedes with certain incomes (information which is public in Sweden). In one other well-known case a German company wanted to transfer the personnel records of its Swedish subsidiary to its German headquarters for automatic processing. Permission was refused because the processing would not then have been subject to any data protection legislation.[40] There seem to be no other reported cases until the summer of 1984, when the Swedish authorities again refused to permit the transfer of personal data for processing outside the country, this time to a company headquarters in Belgium.[41] These are at least examples of how national laws can be barriers, which is the reason for many of the provisions of the Convention. In December 1990 the Data Protection Registrar of the United Kingdom issued a transfer prohibition order forbidding the transfer of personal data to the United States on the ground that US law does not provide adequate protection in the private sector.[42]

The Council of Europe's Convention for the Protection of Individuals with regard to Automatic Processing of Personal Data

Both the Council of Europe's Convention and the OECD Guidelines were adopted and published in 1980, and the Convention was opened for signature on 28 January 1981. The Convention came into effect in 1985, and is now legally binding on its adhering parties, which the Guidelines are not. The Convention has three major functions: it establishes basic rules for data protection measures to be adopted by adhering states; it sets out special rules about transborder data flows; and it establishes mechanisms for consultation, if not enforcement. The Convention is not a 'European' Convention; the absence of 'European' from its formal title emphasises that it is open for adherence and ratification by non-European countries.

The core of principles gives considerable scope for variation to suit different constitutional and legal systems in their domestic implementation. These are found in Chapter II, beginning with the obligation on Parties to take the necessary measures in domestic law to give effect to the principles. 'Measures' is not necessarily limited to laws, but it is unlikely that a domestic approach limited to voluntary codes alone would comply with the Convention. The measures must be in force at the time when the State concerned becomes bound by the Convention. It is, however, open to a country (under Article 3.2(a)) at the time of accession to deposit with the Council of Europe a list of automated personal data files which are not covered by its domestic law, and to which it will not apply the Convention. (Such action could, however, have adverse effects on transborder data flows under Article 12.)

Article 5 sets out the basic principles of data protection, as to both the contents of the data and their processing. If they undergo automatic processing they are to be:

(a)   obtained fairly and lawfully;
(b)   stored for specified and legitimate purposes and not used in a way incompatible with those purposes;
(c)   adequate, relevant and not excessive in relation to the purposes for which they are stored;
(d)   accurate and, where necessary, kept up to date;
(e)   preserved in a form which permits identification of the data subjects for no longer than is required for the purpose for which those data are stored.

This does not attempt to describe for what purposes personal data may be stored, but at least bars the collection of such data for no declared purpose. The last principle probably does not require an irrevocable 'anonymization' of name-linked data, but only adequate security measures.

The 'special categories' of personal data in Article 6 are not to be processed automatically 'unless domestic law provides appropriate safeguards'. The list represents a broad consensus on the sort of personal information regarded as particularly sensitive by representatives of the European countries in the late twentieth century. They are 'personal data revealing racial origin, political opinions or religious or other beliefs, as well as data concerning health or sexual life', and 'the same shall apply to personal data relating to criminal convictions'. This is a minimum list, and it is open to Parties under Article 11 to give effect to cultural values by giving similar special protection to other kinds of personal data. To descend to the particular, the inclusion of criminal convictions in the list will pose problems for newspapers which use or disseminate data from automated databases; it may be an incentive for them to adopt the Swedish practice of not identifying defendants in criminal trials (although the exception to that rule for 'public figures' would seem to violate the principle as well). Article 7 requires 'appropriate security measures'.

Article 8 is about 'additional safeguards for the data subject', but might be better called 'rights of data subjects', except that the Convention does not necessarily require the creation of rights. There is a division in data protection circles between those who see a right such as subject access as one of several means to the end of seeing that personal data are handled according to Article 5 principles, and those who see subject access as an independent right of its own. The article requires domestic legislation to give data subjects the right to know whether there are automated data files on them; to find out the contents of such files; to have errors corrected or deleted; and to have a remedy if these rights are violated. Although the right to know of the existence of files does not require a public register of their controllers, other measures, such as notification to a data subject when the file is opened, would be required to provide equivalent protection. It is not clear from the text whether the right to rectification includes retrospective notification to everyone who has received the erroneous information, but it would seem at least arguable that it does.

None of the data protection principles is absolute. Article 9 attempts to define the circumstances in which states are justified in departing from the principles. The resemblance of the qualifying second paragraph to several of the rights under the European Convention on Human Rights is deliberate. The easiest exception is for personal data files 'used for statistics or for scientific research where there is obviously no risk of an infringement of the privacy of the data subjects'. Less easy is the allowance of derogation from Articles 5, 6, and 8 (the core of the core principles)

> when such derogation is provided for by the law of the Party and constitutes a necessary measure in a democratic society in the interests of:
> (a) protecting state security, public safety, the monetary interests of the state or the suppression of criminal offences;
> (b) protecting the data subject or the rights and freedoms of others.

'Monetary interests' would seem to justify laws to detect tax evasion and violations of exchange controls, and perhaps also violations of social welfare benefits. 'Suppression of criminal offences' may go beyond detection to include at least some elements of prevention. 'Protecting the data subject' is probably intended to justify the reluctance of many medical authorities (and some others) to allow uncontrolled subject access to health data, while one of the major 'rights and freedoms of others' which may conflict with data protection is the right to receive and impart information.

Article 10 states that the domestic methods of implementing the principles must include remedies, while Article 11 makes it clear that the Convention sets basic standards, and that Parties can give greater protection to data subjects, such as rights of access to manual files.

That is the core of requirements to protect the privacy of data subjects. The rest of the Convention is concerned with transborder data flows and machinery for implementation. Article 12 is the key to transborder data flows, defining them as widely as possible, before saying that 'a Party shall not, for the sole purpose of the protection of privacy, prohibit or subject to special authorization transborder flows of personal data going to the territory of another person'. This is the basic rule to prevent national data protection laws having the effect of non-tariff trade barriers on the export of personal data (with imported data coming under the regulation of the importing state), based on the assumption that all Parties to the Convention offer the same basic protection.

Article 12(3) permits derogation from this free information market rule. The first type of derogation is

> in so far as its legislation includes specific regulations for certain categories of personal data or of automated personal data files, because of the nature of those data or those files, except where the regulations of the other Party provide an equivalent protection.

The easier part of this is for those countries which extend their laws to protect legal persons. If those countries have filed a declaration under Article 3.2(b) that they apply the Convention to legal persons, then they may legitimately restrict the export of automated data about legal persons to other countries which give similar protection and have filed the same declaration.

A country may also provide special protection beyond that required by the Convention. This may apply to the type of information, such as the sensitive categories from Article 6 or any other kind of personal information thought to deserve special protection. It may also apply to protection for manual as well as automated files. If appropriate declarations have been filed under Article 3, then the country concerned can legitimately restrict exports of such data to other signatories which do not provide equivalent protection. But exports cannot be restricted to countries which have adopted equivalent special measures.

Article 12 also allows states to limit exports of personal data to other signatory countries if the data are only passing through that country on the way to a non-signatory country. In other words, it is a measure to prevent the 'laundering' of data through one country on the way to a 'data haven' without data protection laws. This is not absolute, however, and it is possible for states which have not signed the Convention to have a system of data protection.

Chapters IV and V establish the machinery and rules for implementation. Article 14 requires the designation of a data protection authority or authorities for the purposes of co-operation with other Parties. The Council of Europe's explanatory note to this section says:

> It should be underlined, however, that while the Convention requires the designation of an authority by each Contracting State, this does not mean that the Convention requires each state to have a data protection authority. A Contracting State may designate an authority for the purposes of the Convention only.

Articles 14 and 15 require equality of treatment for data subjects living abroad, and authorize those data subjects to use the data protection authority of the country where they are living as an intermediary. Article 16 allows refusals of requests for assistance if they ask for something outside the Convention, outside the powers of the recipient data protection authority, or contrary to national security or public policy. Article 17 limits the costs which can be charged for assistance.

Articles 18 to 20 establish a Consultative Committee, which is not given any enforcement powers. Each Party has a representative on the Committee, which is to meet at least once every two years. Its function is not to adjudicate, but to 'make proposals' for the application or amendment of the Convention, and to express an 'opinion' on any proposed amendment or any question concerning the Convention, when requested to do so by a Party. The Committee is clearly expected to assist in the resolution of disputes between Parties, but just as clearly does not have any authority to resolve such disputes formally. In practice, it will be composed largely of representatives of the data protection institutions of the Parties.

Article 21 sets out the procedures for the circulation and approval of amendments, and Article 22 provides that the Convention enters into force three months after the fifth ratification (which in fact occurred in October 1985). Article 23 is potentially one of the most important parts of the Convention: it authorizes accession by countries outside the Council of Europe on the invitation of the Committee of Ministers with the approval of all Parties to the Convention. This is mainly intended for the benefit of the non-European members of the OECD (Canada, USA, Australia and Japan), but there is no reason why other states should not be allowed to accede, providing they are willing to comply with the Convention's provisions.

Article 24 allows states to designate territories to which the Convention will apply. This is particularly important for countries with dependencies on the other side of the globe, such as the United

Kingdom's Hong Kong colony (until 1997), where data processing may be carried out cheaply during non-peak hours. Although Article 25 allows no reservations, a measure of flexibility is already allowed through the permissible derogations under Article 3.

The first five countries to ratify were Sweden, France, Norway, Spain, and West Germany. Of those countries, all except Spain had national data protection laws at the time of ratification. Spain has a constitutional provision, and was in the process of legislating when the bill ran into difficulties in the Cortes.

The OECD Guidelines governing the Protection of Privacy and Transborder Data Flows of Personal Data

The Guidelines are in the language of recommendation rather than obligation, and have special provisions recognising the special problems of federations (such as Canada, the USA, and Australia) and perhaps approving a sectoral approach more than the Convention does. Guideline 5 simply says that: 'In the particular case of Federal countries the observance of these Guidelines may be affected by the division of powers in the Federation.'

Guideline 3 (a) and (b) says:

> These Guidelines should not be interpreted as preventing:
> (a)   the application of different protective measures to different categories of personal data, depending upon their nature and the context in which they are collected, stored, processed or disseminated;
> (b)   the exclusion from the application of the Guidelines of personal data which obviously do not contain any risk to privacy.

The basic principles are similar to those of the Convention, but written in less specific terms. For example, Guideline 13 describes the 'individual participation' of subject access in some detail, including the right to

> have communicated to him, data relating to him
> i.   within a reasonable time;
> ii.   at a charge, if any, that is not excessive;
> iii. in a reasonable manner; and
> iv.   in a form which is readily intelligible to him.

He should also have the right to challenge any denial of a request for such information, and to be given reasons for it. But, unlike the Convention, there is no provision suggesting what reasons, such as national security, are acceptable under the Guidelines for refusing such requests.

The other basic principles in Guidelines 7 to 14 are roughly equivalent to those of the Convention in urging the principles of collection limitation, data quality, purpose specification, use limitation, security safeguards, and accountability. Although the Guidelines do not discuss the question of legal and natural persons, the definition of 'personal data' as 'any information relating to an identified or identifiable individual (data subject)' displays an intention to refer only to natural persons. It would even seem that the Guidelines do not contemplate supplementary measures to cover legal persons, although inclusion of manual records (as in three of the non-European member states) would seem to be within the statement (Guideline 6) that: 'These Guidelines should be regarded as minimum standards which are capable of being supplemented by additional measures for the protection of privacy and individual liberties.'

Part Three of the Guidelines is concerned with ensuring the free flow of information, and indicating permissible barriers. Guideline 15 suggests that countries consider the implications of domestic processing of personal data to circumvent the data protection laws of other countries. This is a diplomatic way of saying that member countries should not be data havens, or assist them. Guidelines 16 and 17 urge uninterrupted flows of personal data between member countries, except for any member which does not 'substantially observe' the Guidelines. No. 18 urges members to

> refrain from developing laws, policies and practices in the name of the protection of privacy and individual liberties which, by exceeding requirements for the protection of privacy and individual liberties, are inconsistent with the free transborder flow of personal data.

This should probably be read in conjunction with Guideline 22, which says that members should 'ensure that procedures for transborder flows of personal data and for the protection of privacy and individual liberties are simple and compatible with those of other Member countries'.

The transborder data flow aspects of the Guidelines were given further emphasis by the OECD Declaration on Transborder Data Flows adopted by the organization's Committee on Information, Computers and Communications on 22 March 1985. Among other things the Declaration considered the Guidelines and 'the significant progress that has been achieved in the area of privacy protection at national and international levels', and declared an intention to 'avoid the creation of unjustified barriers to the international exchange of data and information' and to 'develop common approaches for dealing with issues related to transborder data flows and, when appropriate, develop harmonized solutions'.[43]

The European Community Draft Directive on Data Protection

In 1990 the European Community published a draft directive on data protection. The draft directive followed several years of discussion in which EC states were urged to become parties to the Council of Europe Convention and the Community took steps towards itself becoming party to the Convention. The purpose of the directive was primarily to remove national barriers within the Community to a common market in information, but some attention was paid to the human rights and consumer protection aspects. Several features of the draft directive attracted attention. The provisions of the directive would not be limited to computerized data, but would apply to some systems of manual records. Direct mail organizations and charities argued that the requirement to obtain data subject consent to inclusion would make their activities more difficult. Some journalists, among others, were critical of the absolute ban on the automatic processing of criminal conviction records in the private sector. As of December 1991 it is unclear whether the draft directive will become final, and, if it does, if it will be in the original form. Despite a book on the subject by the late Edward Ploman, there is not yet a recognized body of international law known as 'information law', but there are many specific instruments of international law which may affect, and may be intended to affect, the flow of information across borders. The 1952 Convention on the International Right of Correction (which has collected only very few ratifications) requires Contracting States to publicize corrections of news reports when requested to by other Contracting Parties. The 1948 'Beirut Agreement' for 'facilitating the international circulation of visual and auditory materials of an educational, scientific and cultural character' binds Contracting Parties to exempt such materials from customs restrictions, and is further implemented by the 1950 Florence Agreement and the 1976 Protocol.

Other international instruments

There is a large body of international law relating to telecommunications, of which the most important single instruments are probably the International Telecommunications Convention of 1973, the Telegraph and Telephone Regulations of 1973, and the 1979 Radio Regulations of the World Administration Radio Conference. Other related instruments include the Convention Relating to the Distribution of Programme-carrying Signals Transmitted by Satellite of 1974. The 1964 Constitution of the Universal Postal Union and the Universal Postal Convention of 1974 establish rules for non-electronic international communication.

There are more than 20 conventions and agreements related to intellectual and industrial property. Instruments devoted largely to limiting trade barriers include the General Agreement on Tariffs and Trade (GATT), the Treaty of Rome establishing the European Economic Community, the Convention Establishing a Customs Co-operation Council, and the Convention Establishing the Organization for Economic Co-operation and Development.[44]

Transborder Data Flows

At a British conference, while the United Kingdom Data Protection Bill was being debated in Parliament, one speaker gave the following illustration:

> Let us suppose that one of our major trading partners in Europe, who is also a commercial competitor, is a country called Ruritania. Ruritania has a data protection law in force, and the government of Ruritania would very much like, on commercial and economic grounds, to inhibit the data flows passing between Ruritania and London, perhaps because British insurers are underwriting too much business in Ruritania for the Ruritanian insurance companies' comfort. So the Ruritanian government goes to the Ruritanian Data Protection Commissioner and says,
>   'Look here, you are the expert on this. Is there any way that we could complain that the United Kingdom is in breach of the Data Protection Convention?'
>   'Oh, sure,' he says, 'an exemption for immigration – that's not allowed.'
>   'Ah, great, let's cut off their data flows.'[45]

As it happened, the British government removed the exemption (from the subject access and non-disclosure principles) for information related to immigration control before the Bill was enacted, though not before attempting to justify it under the Convention as being allegedly in the interests of 'the rights and freedoms of others' in the labour market. But the fundamental problem remains: what are the consequences if one country, in the interests of data protection, limits transborder data flows to another country, when both countries are Parties to the Council of Europe's Data Protection Convention?

A more elaborate version of this hypothetical example was published in 1981.[46] The author there suggested alternative solutions for a US company, both intriguing. In the absence of US legislation equivalent to that in many European countries, he suggested that a US company could bind itself contractually to observe the data protection law of the European data exporter, or that the parties could agree, in a choice-of-law clause, for the exporter's data protection law to apply. As mentioned earlier, in December 1990 the British Data Protection Registrar prohibited the transfer to the United States by a British data user of personal data on the ground that US private sector law did not provide adequate protection. The order was not appealed to the Data Protection Tribunal, and seems to have attracted little attention apart from one article.[47]

In considering the problem it will be assumed that such action would be taken entirely in the interests of data protection, and that any benefit to the domestic informatics industry would be unintended. It is also assumed that the restriction does not violate any other international agreement, such as those on posts and telecommunications, not to impede the free flow of information. The legal question would be whether such a country was acting within the justifiable derogations under the Convention, which could, in turn, depend on whether the derogations of recipient countries were justified under the Convention.[48]

The procedural, or practical, question would be what body could decide such a dispute. The Consultative Committee could express an opinion if requested, but that would not have any binding force. It has been suggested that the institutions of the European Convention on Human Rights might have jurisdiction, on the theory that the Data Protection Convention is a particular application of the right to privacy under the Human Rights Convention. (The suggestion was made by Judge Pettiti, of the European Court of Human Rights, during a Council of Europe conference on data protection in Madrid in June 1984.)[49]

If that were to happen – and it now seems very unlikely – it would almost certainly be by way of an inter-state application to the Commission, with the country imposing the restrictions arguing that it is not in breach of its obligations under the Data Protection Convention because the recipient country is in breach of both the Data Protection and the Human Rights Conventions. Even if both countries were members of the Council of Europe the matter would present difficulties. But if one of the countries were a non-European signatory to the Data Protection Convention it would be impossible.

A case which illustrates the potential for such conflict was that of the database of the fire brigade in Malmö, Sweden, which was physically located in the State of Ohio, in the USA. Because the database had some personal information, the Swedish Data Inspection Board refused permission to continue using the facilities in Ohio because there was no federal or state data protection law covering the private sector there.[50] If that were to happen now, and if the USA had been allowed to adhere to the Convention, the likely route would be by way of a request for an opinion from the Consultative Committee. If that failed, the good offices of the OECD could doubtless be enlisted. If those failed too, it would be a matter for international negotiation rather than adjudication. As the country reports below show, there are broadly differing approaches to data protection. On the question of whether there should be a broad regulation of the private sector, for instance, there are two general approaches: the European countries which have legislated generally favour it; those which do not include Canada, the USA, Australia and Japan.

For these non-European countries the OECD Guidelines are a step in the direction of comprehensive regulation of the public and private sectors, although not as specific and binding as the Convention. They are clearly seen as a method of avoiding national barriers to transborder data flows. After Canada agreed to follow the Guidelines in June 1984, the Foreign Minister sent a letter to about 150 Canadian companies, urging them to comply with the Guidelines. In it he said:

> If the private sector does not take action to implement the Guidelines, there is a risk that other OECD countries could restrict or prohibit the flow of personal data to Canada. This clearly would have adverse economic consequences for Canadian businesses.[51]

Information is both an economic good and a subject matter of human rights, and these two aspects create many of the problems in transborder data flows. (Information is not unique in this duality, however; the freedom to cross frontiers for work has certain similarities.) To complicate matters further, there are at least two further distinct characteristics within the aspects of human rights and economics. As a human right, in the words of all the general human rights instruments, individuals are entitled both to 'receive' and to 'impart' information. Traditional formulations of the right to freedom of expression have concentrated, at least so far as they have been formulated in law, on the rights of individuals not to be unduly restricted in what they say. It is now being realized, however, and increasingly expressed in legal norms, that the readers deprived of a censored book have their rights violated just as much as its author, to take just one example. One consequence of this is a shift in emphasis from the 'freedom' or 'liberty' of expression to the 'right' both to impart and to receive information – a right coming to be known as 'the right to communicate'. A freedom implies a relative absence of restrictions, particularly legal restrictions imposed by the state. A right of any sort implies a correlative duty; in the case of information the duties can include the provision of access, without discrimination, to the media of communication, both for those who wish to impart and those who wish to receive information.

Information is both capable of commercial value and yet incapable of being 'stolen' in the sense that tangible property is when someone is deprived permanently of its possession or use. The entire law of intellectual property is an attempt to recognize the commercial value and establish rights over the control and exploitation of this intangible 'commodity'.[52] The formulation of rules which treat information as a commodity may lead to results which appear counterintuitive: copyright and patent laws are restrictions on the exploitation of information by the general public. The ostensible, and usually real, reason for these restrictions is to provide a sufficient incentive to produce new forms of information and associated other goods, on the assumption that such innovations are likely to benefit society. The restrictions are in the form of statutory monopolies for limited periods, and usually require that the information be made public in exchange for protection against its exploitation by others.

Although information is a 'commodity' which is 'produced', 'distributed', and 'consumed', its essentially intangible character makes all these words mean rather different things than when they are used in association with tangible commodities. The production of information may cost a great deal in material terms. The distribution is really reproduction, which may cost very little. The consumption by reception of information does not by itself deprive others of the possibility of similar consumption. Many restrictions on communication of information are, as in the case of copyright, artificial limits to enhance market value, as a substitute for other mechanisms, such as supply and demand, in markets for tangibles.

Information is not, however, just a commodity, however intangible. It is also the subject of the human rights described above, which, in terms of international law, have been recognized since the Second World War. These human rights represent a significant change from what was previously called 'the law of nations': they confer status and rights on individuals as well as nations. Less immediately obvious in the case of the various formulations of the right to receive and impart information, but of vital importance for transborder data flows, is the fact that all these formulations (with the single exception of the American Declaration of the Rights and Duties of Man) proclaim the right 'regardless of frontiers'.

There were international instruments regulating transborder data flows before the Second World War, but they were concerned with the rights and obligations of nations (usually reciprocal), and were designed to facilitate the advancement of national objectives through the harmonization of standards. They recognized individuals only obliquely, and there was little in their content to further the individual human right to receive and impart information across national borders.

The recognition in international law of both the status of individuals and their right to receive and impart information across frontiers has been accompanied by a massive shift in economic activity from goods to information. There lies the test of the relationship between information privacy and transborder data flows. The value assigned to privacy is reflected in restrictions on the free flow of information. Both the free flow of information and personal privacy are fundamental human values, and they sometimes conflict. Without digressing into natural law and instrumental theories for these values, it can be said that one function of the free flow of information is to benefit the world community through a free market in information and ideas. Although the enforcement of a right to personal privacy may restrict a completely free flow, this restriction can be seen as compatible with the purpose of a (social) market-place for ideas if it functions to cultivate the imagination and invention of the individual human personality (expressed in similar words in Article 2(1) of the German constitution). Thus, the harmonization of national standards about data protection is pursued not just for the purpose of reducing their potential to act as non-tariff trade barriers, any more than agreements on product safety standards are pursued simply to promote trade. Both also have the purpose of reflecting the values of protecting personal privacy, and personal safety, respectively.[53]

An international commitment to the free flow of information should recognize the specific interests which may justify restrictions on that flow, and provide mechanisms for the resolution of conflicts between those interests and the free flow of information. International human rights instruments such as the Universal Declaration, the International Covenant, and the European Convention have specified interests which justify restrictions, one of which is the protection of personal privacy. The Data Protection Convention of the Council of Europe and the OECD Guidelines are attempts at defining the content of information privacy, particularly as it is affected by technology. Their purpose is not, or should not be, only to reduce potential barriers to the free flow of information, but also to establish common standards of data protection within their information markets.

Restrictions on transborder data flows in the interests of protecting personal privacy can be justified under the Covenant on Civil and Political Rights as being provided for by law and necessary 'for the respect of the rights or reputations of others'. The Covenant is more liberal than the European Convention on Human Rights in having only two such limitations, the other being 'for the protection of national security or of public order, or of public health or morals'. Article 10 of the European Convention has a more detailed list of justifiable restrictions on the right to receive and impart information. These are similar, but not identical, to the justifiable restrictions on the right to privacy under Article 8. Freedom of expression may be justified by law if it is necessary in a democratic society in the interests of

> national security, territorial integrity or public safety, for the prevention of disorder or crime, for the protection of health or morals, for the protection of the reputation or rights of others, for preventing the disclosure of information received in confidence, or for maintaining the authority and impartiality of the judiciary.

Restrictions on the free flow of information between Council of Europe countries may thus be justified so far as is necessary, but no more, to protect 'the reputations or rights of others'.

The OECD thus far has emphasized the economic importance of a world-wide free flow of information, and has been rather less specific about the human rights aspects, both in the right to receive and impart information and in the right to privacy which may justify barriers to the free flow. In 1983 a declaration of human rights oriented principles for transborder data flow was proposed to the OECD Expert Party on Transborder Data Flows, but not circulated for open discussion.[54] It would have declared, among other things, a policy:

> (1)   to respect the right to freedom of expression by individuals and associations, without discrimination of any kind, as recognized in international law;

> (2)   to impose no prior censorship or any arbitrary controls or constraints on participants in legitimate flows of information;

> (3)   while recognizing that the right to freedom of expression carries with it special duties and responsibilities, to confine any restrictions on it strictly to those authorized by international law where that is necessary to protect national security, public order, public health or morals, or respect for the rights and reputations of others, including their right not to be subjected to arbitrary or unlawful interference with their privacy, family, home or correspondence, nor to unlawful attacks on their honour or reputation, and their right to benefit from the protection of the moral and material interests resulting from any scientific, literary or artistic production of which they are the authors;

> (4)   to encourage the development and establishment of a wide variety of independent and autonomous providers of information, information services and communication channels, in order to allow the widest possible freedom of choice for those seeking to communicate or receive information;

> (5)   to provide fair and equitable access on reasonable terms to such information, information services and communication channels, and

opportunities to participate in them and in the formulation, application, monitoring and review of information and communication policies, at all relevant levels and at all stages;

(6) to make available such access to those who wish to exercise any other of their rights and freedoms protected by international law, including the rights to health, education, assembly and association, to take part in public affairs and cultural life, to enjoy the benefits of scientific progress and its applications, and the freedom indispensable for scientific research and creative activity;

(7) to make available an adequate right of reply and correction to anyone who has been injured by inaccurate and offensive statements disseminated to the public;

(8) to ensure that all improvements in information and communication technology are used to support and extend, and not to restrict or narrow, the rights to freedom of expression and the principle of the unrestricted flow of information;

(9) to respect the cultures of different nations and peoples while encouraging their mutual enrichment.

Paragraph (3) of this proposed declaration is of particular relevance to the present study because it is concerned with the restraints which could be imposed in the interests of protecting privacy. This is based on the declarations of the right to privacy in the Universal Declaration, the UN Covenant, and the European Convention on Human Rights. Its emphasis is clearly different from that of the draft declaration on international data flow submitted to the OECD by the USA in January 1982. That draft provided for agreement on co-operation, consultation, and encouraging innovation, with determination to improve an open system of international information flows and to avoid restrictive measures; but it did not mention human rights, either to information or to privacy. A draft French proposal for a World Charter of Communications, presented to the 1982 Versailles summit meeting, was based on five principles:

(1) affirming the respect for the diversity of languages;

(2) promoting the harmonization of legislation governing information, intellectual property, contract law, and the protection of individual liberties;

(3) inciting to the determination of common rules for international data exchanges;

(4)   protecting the sovereignty of states and their cultural integrity, which is threatened by the new technologies;

(5)   enabling the countries of the South to control their communications and the messages of which they are the vehicles.

Although the second principle includes individual liberties, this declaration also seems to be primarily urging harmonization, and is more deferential to national and linguistic sovereignty than the US draft. At the least, it would seem that more consideration should be paid to the human rights as well as the economic aspects of transborder data flow, if only for the purposes of resolving the occasional conflicts between the fundamentally complementary human rights to information and privacy.

Notes

1   Samuel Warren, who wrote the seminal *Harvard Law Review* article 'The Right to Privacy' in 1890 with Louis Brandeis, might have approved; the publicity given to his daughter's wedding inspired him to write, and his objection was at least in part on behalf of his family.
2   Volio, Fernando (1981), 'Legal Personality, Privacy, and the Family', in Henkin (ed.), *The International Bill of Rights*, New York: Columbia University Press.
3   13 GAOR Annexes, UN Doc. A/405 para. 46 (1958).
4   International Commission of Jurists (1967), *The Rule of Law and Human Rights: Principles and Definitions*, pp. 63–4.
5   Novoa, E. (1977), *Derecho a la Vida y la Libertad de Información, un Conflicto de Derechos*, pp. 45–6.
6   33 GAOR Supp. 40, UN Doc. A/33/40 para. 348, 239, (1978).
7   Verdoodt, A. (1964), *Naissance et Signification de la Déclaration Universelle des Droits de L'Homme*, Louvain and Paris: Editions Nauwelserts, pp. 138–43.
8   Resolution 2450 of 19 December 1968, UN Doc. E/CN. 4/1025.
9   Document E/CN. 4/1116.
10   Cmnd. 5012, para. 53.
11   Document E/CN. 4/1233, 1976.
12   *André Deklerck v. Belgium*, Application No. 8307/78, DR 21, p. 116.
13   Application No. 6825/74, DR 5, p. 86, and see below, p. 93.
14   The right of individual petition has now been accepted, although not always for the same period of years, by all the States Parties.
15   Case Law Topics Number 1, 'Human Rights in Prison', Council of Europe: Strasbourg, pp. 23–4 (1970).
16   No. 8231/78, *X v. United Kingdom*, Vol. 28 D&R, pp. 38–9; No. 8166/78, *X & Y v. Switzerland*, Vol. 13 D&R, p. 243.
17   As in No. 2749/66, *DeCourcy v. United Kingdom*, 10 Yearbook 412.
18   No. 4451/70, judgment of 21 February 1975, Series A, No. 18.
19   Judgment of 28 June 1984, Series A, No. 80.
20   *Klass v. Federal Republic of Germany*, judgment of 6 September 1978, Series A, No. 28 paras 30–8.
21   *International Social Science Journal*, Vol. XXIV, No. 3, 1972, p. 507.

22 *Smith* v. *Maryland*, 99 S.Ct. 2577, in which obtaining information by use of a 'pen-register' (metering) was held not to violate the right to privacy.

23 Application No. 5877/72, *X* v. *United Kingdom*, CD 45 p. 90.

24 Application No. 1307/61, *X* v. *Federal Republic of Germany*, CD 9, p. 53.

25 Application No. 8170/78, *X* v. *Austria*, DR 16 p. 145.

26 Application 10/1985/96/144, judgment of 26 March 1987, Series A No. 116.

27 Judgment of 7 July 1989, Series A No. 160.

28 Application No. 9702/82, *X* v. *United Kingdom*, decision of 6 October 1982.

29 The application was, however, rejected because the applicant had not exhausted domestic remedies. Commission opinion of 1 March 1979, para. 52.

30 *Dudgeon* v. *United Kingdom*, judgment of 22 October 1981, Series A, No. 45. *Norris* v. *Ireland*, 1988.

31 No. 7215/75, *X* v. *United Kingdom*, Vol. 19 D&R, p. 66.

32 410 US 113 (1973).

33 No. 6959/75, *Brüggemann and Scheuten* v. *Federal Republic of Germany*, Vol. 10 D&R, p. 100.

34 *Marckx* v. *Belgium*, judgment of 13 June 1979, Series A, No. 31.

35 No. 509.

36 Resolution (73)22 'On the Protection of the Privacy of Individuals *vis-à-vis* Electronic Data Banks in the Private Sector', adopted 26 September 1973; and Resolution (74)29, adopted 24 September 1974.

37 No. 890.

38 See below, p. 145.

39 Cmnd. 7341, para. 27.16, note (1).

40 'Agencies of Data Protection and the Control of Transborder Data Flows', unpublished paper by Herbert Burkert, Gesellschaft für Mathematik und Datenverarbeitung, Cologne, Federal Republic of Germany, pp. 7–9.

41 Transnational Data Reporting Service newsletter, July 1984.

42 'Whose File Is It Anyway?', *Solicitors Journal*, 15 March 1991, Vol. 135, No. 10, pp. 304–5.

43 *Transnational Data Report*, Vol. VIII, No. 3 (April/May 1985), pp. 115–17.

44 For the texts of these and other instruments, see Ploman, E.W. (1982), *International Law Governing Communications and Information*, London: Francis Pinter.

45 Sieghart, P., in Bourn, C. and Benyon, J. (eds), *Data Protection: Perspectives on Information Privacy*, transcript of a conference on 11 May 1983 at the University of Leicester.

46 Epperson, G.M. (1981), 'Contracts for Transnational Information Services: Securing Equivalency of Data Protection', 22 *Harvard International Law Journal*, 157.

47 'Whose File Is It Anyway?', *Solicitors Journal*, 15 March 1991, Vol. 135 No 10, pp. 304–5.

48 See Nugter, A.C.M. (1990), *Transborder Flow of Personal Data within the EC*, Deventer: Kluwer Law and Taxation Publishers.

49 Proceedings of the Conference on the Problems relating to Legislation in the Field of Data Protection held in Madrid (1984), published by the Council of Europe, Strasbourg, Doc. DP/CONF. 84/1, 2 and 3.

50 *Data Protection: Perspectives on Information Privacy*, pp. 31–2.

51 *Transnational Data Report*, Vol. VIII, No. 5 (July/August 1985), p. 243.

52 See Sieghart, P. (1982), 'Information Technology and Intellectual Property', *European Intellectual Property Review*, July.

53 See Sieghart, P. (1981), 'The International Implications of the Development of Micro-electronics', *The Information Society*, Vol. 1, No. 1.

54 *Transnational Data Report*, Vol. VI, No. 6 (September 1983), pp. 293–9.

3   Country Reports

Countries with National Data Protection Laws and Access to Government Information Laws

Sweden

As has already been noted, Sweden was the first country to legislate nationally on data protection,[1] and has served as something of a model, not only for the other Nordic countries but for other countries in Europe and beyond, in dealing with the problems of computers and privacy. What is perhaps less well known is that Sweden has long had a constitutional principle that is in a sense the converse of personal privacy in redressing the balance of power between the individual and the state: Sweden was the first country, by exactly two centuries, to enact a national law providing a general right of access to official documents.[2]

Swedish authorities often suggest that there was a causal relationship between these two laws. However, they did not develop quite as symmetrically as such a relationship might suggest, particularly regarding the protection of personal privacy. The access to information law, included in the Freedom of the Press Act but not limited to the press, was passed after a faction known as the 'Caps' (*mössorna*) gained power over the 'Hats' (*hattarna*). It has been suggested that there was an even older principle that Swedish administrative affairs had to be dealt with in public, and that this had become less important during the 'Age of Liberty' (1718–72). It does seem clear that the principle of open government (*offentlighetsprincip*) was established in association with provisions abolishing censorship. This liberal regime ended with Gustav III's seizure of power in 1772, and was not re-established until after the revolution of 1809. The Freedom of the Press Act was then adopted as part of the Constitution, including other provisions such as the 'anonymity principle' which generally protects the confidentiality of sources for journalists, although it was included more to protect the anonymity of pamphleteers. Whatever the reasons for these enactments, they were probably not primarily to establish a right of 'subject access' in order to protect that aspect of privacy which we now call data protection. They were, and are, used by data subjects to gain access to official documents which concern them, especially when the documents are manual ones which are not subject to the subject access provisions of the Data Law, and the existence of this right is sometimes referred to by Swedish officials when explaining why their country was the first to adopt a Data Protection Act. The ancient principle had certainly been held to apply to computerized records, and the major innovation of the Data Protection Act was to superimpose a system of administrative supervision on the right of subject access.

Despite the long-standing principle and the pioneering legislation, Sweden previously, and perhaps even now, has little law that could be described as a general right to privacy. The 1972 study referred to the comparative study of privacy by Stromholm prepared for the Nordic Conference, and noted two other articles that had been published about privacy. Yet another article, by Professor Logdberg, may illustrate the Swedish legal approach to privacy.[3] It is a comparative study of 'The Right to a Person's Own Likeness', and the section on Swedish law sounds remarkably like a discussion of English law (which is also covered). The approach is not based on a general right to privacy which is considered to be infringed by an 'appropriation of likeness'. Instead, the discussion considers the law of copyright, trademarks, unfair competition, and libel (noting that the equivalent penal rules in Norway were described as 'concerning privacy'). Although Sweden has been quick to perceive a threat to privacy from computers and to deal with it, traditional notions of privacy have thus relied on particular remedies for particular wrongs.

The Freedom of the Press Act, which includes the basic right of public access to government records, has seven very general principles that exempt documents from access, and these principles are elaborated in greater detail in the Secrecy Act. One of these specific exemptions (section 7) is to protect the personal circumstances of individuals. This does not, however, bar the right of access by individuals to documents containing information about themselves but not about others. The general test for refusing access to individuals for files about themselves is that of 'harm'. For example, subject access to records may be refused to medical records if it is considered that it might be harmful, and the same rule applies to social welfare records. This also covers the possibility that access might result in harm to others, especially those closely related to the person seeking access.[4] However, the same section bars secrecy about a decision to take someone into care. There is also an exemption from subject access for reasons of national security (Freedom of the Press Act, section 2(14)), and such decisions are generally made by the relevant minister rather than the courts.

The provision for decisions to withold personal information from the person concerned to be made by a minister is an exception to the usual procedure. A citizen who has been refused access to most government documents, including those concerning him, has two possible avenues of appeal, and need not necessarily choose between them. The more legalistic route is by way of appeal to the Supreme Administrative Court. A less formal method is by complaint to the ombudsman (*justitieombudsman*, or JO) concerned with such complaints. The JO can publicize his decision, but he has no power to make a binding ruling.

The remedies for a Swedish citizen seeking access to information concerning him which is withheld in the interests of national security are now being considered by the institutions of the European Convention on Human Rights in the *Leander* case. That case concerns a Swedish carpenter who was hired by the naval museum, and then dismissed and told that the dismissal was for reasons of national security. His claim is that the refusal of the authorities to provide him with access to the information on which this decision was based was a violation of his right to privacy under Article 8 of the Convention, his right to 'receive and impart information' under Article 10, and his right to an effective remedy for violations of his rights under Article 13.

In such a highly automated country as Sweden, it seems strange that nothing was said in the Commission's report in the *Leander* case to indicate that the national security information had been processed automatically. If it had been so processed, the Data Inspection Board might have become involved, and no reference was made to it. The DIB is the enforcement body established under the Data Protection Act, which was amended in 1982. The DIB administers a system of licences and permissions for the establishment of files of personal information in the private sector. Formal permission is required if the personal information is sensitive, and so might present a threat to privacy. The DIB also regulates the collection of personal information in the public sector.

The DIB's authority is not limited to the Data Protection Act. It also issues licences and supervises two other statutes that may also be considered to be privacy protection measures. These are the Credit Information Act of 1974 and the Debt Recovery Act of the same year. The first of these is roughly equivalent to the US Fair Credit Reporting Act of 1970 and the British Consumer Credit Act of 1974, although the methods of enforcing the three are different. The Swedish Credit Information Act operates both by requiring licences for credit information businesses, including both automatic and manual files, and by establishing a right of subject access. This is more similar to the British law than that of the USA, including both regulation and self-help. The Debt Recovery Act is also closer to the British system than to the US law.

Although Sweden has influenced the world by its data protection legislation, it seems not to have developed any generalized privacy protection law. In this it resembles the United Kingdom, in some instances even more than it resembles other Scandinavian countries. In data protection it continues to revise its legislation. Amendments that came into force in 1988 provided a right to compensation for damage caused by the setting up of an unlicensed system and gave the Data Inspection Board authority to issue regulations on the correction of incorrect or misleading personal data. In August 1990 a Data Legislation Commission was established to make a thorough review of the Data Act and draft a new law. The earliest that the new legislation could come into force is 1993.

Denmark

Denmark followed Sweden in legislating on both access to government information and data protection, taking the same action at almost exactly the same time as did Norway. But there had been earlier elements of Danish law that could be called privacy protection measures. Article 72 of the Constitution protects aspects of both physical and information privacy in saying that:

> The dwelling shall be inviolable. House searching, seizure, and examination of letters and other papers as well as any breach of the secrecy to be observed in postal, telegraph, and telephone matters shall take place only under a judicial order unless particular exception is warranted by statute.

Under Danish law the European Convention on Human Rights was not incorporated into domestic law, although the courts have adopted a 'rule of presumption' that legislation is to be interpreted in conformity with the Convention unless there is an express indication to the contrary.[5]

Danish legal writers were greatly influenced by German theorists who argued for the concept of a general 'personality right'. In one respect, the Danish courts followed this theory to reach a conclusion remarkably like the tort described by Dean Prosser in the USA as the 'appropriation of likeness'. In 1965 the Danish Supreme Court held that, although there was no specific statutory provision to support the ruling, the law should protect an individual against the unauthorized use of the 'good will value of his picture'.[6]

Although it may soon be amended, the access to government information law only applies to non-electronic 'documents'. It covers all such documents held by central or local administrative bodies. In the exemptions from subject access and the procedure for enforcing it, the Danish law is very like those of Sweden and Norway. There is a relatively broad national security exemption and a similar one for information involving the prosecution of criminal offences. For public employees, there is a separate exemption for information relating to appointments and promotions.[7] There is also a familiar exemption to protect the privacy of other individuals. The Danish Act has been criticized for the breadth of its exemptions, or at least for their potential scope. Section 4 empowers ministers to make administrative regulations exempting classes of documents from the access provisions, and there is an overriding exemption to deny access to protect unnamed interests 'where the special circumstances of the matter make secrecy necessary'. However, one Danish authority has argued that this general power is rarely used.[8] Like many recent access to government information laws, it does not apply to documents created before the Act came into effect in 1971. As in Sweden, there is a choice of appeals between the ombudsman and the courts, except that any judicial review is carried out by the ordinary courts instead of special administrative ones.

The Danish data protection law has some novel features, not all of which are specifically relevant to individual privacy. There are two separate laws regulating data protection in the public and the private sectors, both enacted at the same time. The law regulating the private sector covers automated personal information and also some manual files, whereas only automated information is covered in the public sector law.[9] Like the Norwegian law, the Danish gives rights to both natural and legal persons.

In the public sector the Data Surveillance Authority has an advisory role in the establishment of personal registers, and enforces the rights of subject access and deletion or correction of wrong or incomplete data. In the private sector there was no similar general right of access until the law was amended to comply with the Convention; instead, there were rights of subject access to particular types of information (such as that held by credit reference bureaux), and a requirement that the processing of 'sensitive' personal data can only be done after notice to and with the consent of the person concerned. Because there was no general right of subject access in the private sector it was thought that Denmark might not be wholly in compliance with the Council of Europe's Data Protection Convention. The law was amended to provide such a general right, followed by Denmark's ratification of the Convention.

In September 1991 the Public Authorities Registers Act was amended to reflect the rapid spread of personal computers in the public sector and to reduce the formal requirements for approving their use for processing personal data. Statutory instruments are no longer required to establish such files, but they must still be reported to the Data Surveillance Authority. The rules on access to medical files were changed to give data subjects a direct right of access rather than through a doctor.

Norway

Norway did not legislate to establish a public right of access to government records until 1970 when, after a long-standing controversy similar to that in Denmark, it finally acted.[10] Eight years later it passed a data protection law, although this did not come into effect until 1980.[11] Both these laws, like those in Sweden, provide a right of subject access to records.

The Norwegian constitution does not provide for a right of privacy, except in the provision of Article 102 that 'Search of private homes shall not be made except in criminal cases.' As Norway adheres to the dualist theory of international and domestic law, the European Convention on Human Rights is not directly enforceable in Norwegian courts. However, the Convention has considerable persuasive influence over both administrative and judicial interpretation.[12]

There have been occasional decisions by Norwegian courts which approach the sort of privacy law-making that US judges have engaged in. For example, in 1952 a film about a convicted, but long rehabilitated, murderer was banned.[13] The decision resembles the 'red kimono' case in the USA, in which a Californian court protected the privacy of a rehabilitated prostitute by awarding damages for a portrayal of her earlier life.[14]

The Norwegian law on public access to government documents seems, potentially at least, to be a less effective measure for protecting personal privacy by subject access than the Swedish equivalent. For example, an explanatory memorandum issued by the Justice Department interpreted the new law restrictively (rather like the first US Attorney-General's memorandum interpreting the Freedom of Information Act after it was passed in 1966). The memorandum included a comment that access could be refused to 'the mentally ill, inebriates, small children, rowdies, and slanderers'.[15] The law does not apply to documents created before it came into effect, and the right of access is subject to very wide exemptions. For example, sections 4 and 11 permit the government to exempt classes of documents by decree, and section 4 also permits administrative agencies to refuse access to documents if they would give an 'obviously misleading picture of the case'.

There is also an exemption to protect information that would affect the privacy of others, unless the consent of such other people is obtained. The 1982 amendment established something like the 'third-party procedure' under equivalent Canadian legislation, under which a department receiving a request for access to records concerning a third party must give notice. If no answer is received it is considered to be a denial of consent.[16]

The procedure for appealing against refusals of access is similar to that in Sweden, by complaint to the ombudsman, but differs in that judicial appeals are taken to the ordinary courts. Perhaps because of its wide exemptions, it seems not to have been used much as a method of subject access. Unlike the Swedish law, it has been interpreted not to apply to computerized data. However, one provision of the 1982 amendment was to authorize regulations to include in the definition of 'document' information stored by electronic means, and a research project at the Norwegian Centre for Computers and Law is being carried out to draft such a regulation.

The Norwegian data protection law protects the privacy of both natural and legal persons. It applies to both automated and manual registers, and to both the public and private sectors. It includes special regulations for the processing of sensitive personal information, and has particular provisions for the regulation of certain sectors of the information industry, such as credit reference bureaux, opinion pollsters, and direct mail businesses.

The extensive licensing provisions of the law were somewhat difficult to implement at first, and there were complaints that insufficient funds had been provided.[17] The law is enforced by the Data Inspectorate (*Datailsynet*). It has exemptions from the principle of subject access, but they seem more limited than the exemptions to the law on access to documents. There is an exemption similar to that in the Swedish law by which access may be refused for reasons of the health of the requester or a member of the requester's family, and there is a power for the Inspectorate to exempt systems of records involving law enforcement, defence, or tax administration. The right of subject access has annexed to it a right to have information corrected if it is erroneous, or deleted if it is incorrect or irrelevant.

Two cases illustrate how the Data Inspectorate can enforce rights of subject access, and perhaps also show some limits to the Inspectorate's powers. In August 1982 the Inspectorate examined a social security report after the subject complained that it was unfair. The Inspectorate found that the report did not distinguish between facts and judgements, and did not indicate the sources of information used. The report was destroyed. Another case arose in the autumn of

1983 when the police searched the offices of the Norwegian War Resistance Movement after its newspaper had carried articles about defence installations. Membership and subscriber lists were taken and later returned, but the organization complained to the Inspectorate that copies had been made by the Norwegian security services. After consultation the Ministry of Justice said that the Inspectorate could not intervene in the work of the police while an investigation was under way, although it would have a right to inspect police files after the case was closed.[18]

Finland

In a general way, the Constitution of Finland guarantees some aspects of the right to privacy. Article 6 says that 'Every Finnish citizen shall be protected by law as to life, honour, personal liberty and property.' Article 12 provides that 'The secrecy of postal, telegraphic and telephonic communications shall be inviolable, unless exceptions are provided by law.' It also has had an access to government information act since 1951, although it is not, as its Swedish equivalent is, a part of the constitution.

Finland is a member of the Nordic Council and, although it was the first to follow Sweden in adopting an access to information law, will now be the last to adopt data protection legislation. The need for data protection, or at least for amendment of the access law, was made more acute by a decision of the Supreme Administrative Court that computerized data were not within the law's definition of 'document'. Otherwise, the definition of document is similar to that in Sweden: they are final when signed or when received in the department and noted in a register.

The law applies to all such documents held by public authorities, which excludes information about many activities such as social services which may be carried out by 'private' organizations. The right of access is limited to Finnish citizens, and is only to the production of copies of documents, which does not include the right to inspect them before copying The enforcement mechanism is very like that in Sweden, with the alternative of complaints to the ombudsman, whose recommendations do not have the force of orders, but are very persuasive, and appeals to the administrative courts and the Supreme Administrative Court.

The exemptions include a special provision for the protection of privacy. Apart from that there are the two classes similar to those under many other access laws: documents which must be kept secret and documents which are exempt from disclosure but which may be subject to discretionary disclosure. The mandatory exemptions are for documents related to national security, defence, law enforcement, and 'internal' documents. There is an extraordinary power for the government to refuse access to a document even though it is not exempt under existing law.

The exemptions in the interests of personal privacy include particular provisions for notations on spiritual guidance or church discipline, memoranda in prisons, reformatories, custodial institutions or hospitals, medical certificates, and other comparable records.[19] Personal letters not related to court proceedings are also exempt from disclosure when they are in the possession of public authorities.[20] Such documents will only be released with the consent of the person concerned, although there seems to be no statutory procedure for notification of the person concerned to consider the weight of the privacy interest or a consent to waive it. In one case the ombudsman upheld an authority that refused to release personal records concerning a wife to her husband without her consent.[21] Documents remain exempt for 20 years after the death of the person concerned.[22] It seems that this notion of privacy is extended to legal persons, and that disclosure of documents concerning a legal person must be with the company's consent.[23]

There is a relatively high level of automation of personal data in the country. The Finnish State Computer Centre was established in 1964 to process the population register and other data processing applications. The register, like those in other Scandinavian countries, is still based on local church registers, and it includes considerable personal information. It also is used as a base for other files such as driving licences and social security.

Consciousness of data protection issues is relatively high, and steps were taken to introduce voluntary guidelines. A data protection commission report in 1972 included a series of recommendations similar to the principles being developed elsewhere. The drafting of proposed legislation was left to another group, the Data Systems Committee, which reported in 1975.

Finland passed a Personal Data Files Act in 1987, which came into force on 1 January 1988. It covers both automated and manual records, applies to natural persons, and covers both the public and private sectors. It establishes a Data Protection Board, which may give permission for the export of sensitive data to countries without equivalent legislation. It also establishes a Data Protection Ombudsman, and requires companies to notify the ombudsman if they process certain types of name-linked personal data. As in amendments to legislation in other Scandinavian countries the law substitutes a simple declaration for data users who only process less-sensitive data. Finland, now a member of the Council of Europe, signed the Council of Europe Data Protection Convention on 10 April 1991.

The Netherlands

The Constitution of the Netherlands did not include a general right to privacy until 1983, although there were particular provisions to protect some privacy rights. The 1983 Constitution sets forth a general right to privacy in Article 10. This is subject to limitations by legislation, and allows a ten-year period for legislation to implement the right. The implementing legislation is to include provisions regarding personal registration and a right of subject access and correction. Article 11 specifically recognizes a right to physical privacy, subject to legislative qualification. Article 12 reinforces the right to privacy in the home by requiring officers who enter to present credentials. The right to postal secrecy is extended to telephone conversations.[24] Article 173 provides that the secrecy of letters shall be 'inviolable, except by order of a judge in cases provided for by law', and Article 172 protects physical privacy by allowing the entry of a dwelling against the occupant's will only 'in the cases determined by law, by virtue of a special or general order given by an authority designated by law'. But the incorporation of the European Convention on Human Rights into Dutch law is potentially more important. The importance of the privacy provisions in the Dutch Constitution is diminished by the prohibition in Article 131 of judicial review of statutes. Those rights thus do not provide authority for any Dutch equivalent to most US Supreme Court case law on privacy. The Convention apparently does, because Articles 65 and 66 provide that treaty provisions which are directly applicable are self-executing, and that the courts are not only allowed, but may be required, to overrule domestic statutes that conflict with such provisions. This authority has not yet been exercised in cases involving the right to privacy under the Convention, although Dutch courts have referred to the Convention and decisions interpreting it (even decisions by the Commission on admissibility) in considering objections to domestic statutes.[25]

The Netherlands was something of an exception to the general trend in Europe for data protection legislation combined with less enthusiasm for access to information laws. The country has had an access to information law since 1978 but, despite public concern and many bills, delayed adopting data protection legislation until 1988. In this respect it resembled Finland, although the Netherlands was more susceptible to pressure as a member both of the European Community and the Council of Europe. (Finland has only recently joined the Council and become party to the Data Protection Convention.)

This may have been a product of concern about data protection rather than an indication that attention has not been paid to the subject. There was even more concern in the Netherlands than in other countries at the time of the 1971 census, which was the first to be processed by computers. Protest committees were formed, many refused to co-operate in the census, and plans to keep 10 per cent of the returns for further research were dropped. A Royal Commission on Privacy, commonly known as the Koopmans Commission, was appointed in 1972. It reported in 1972 and 1976, including a draft data protection bill in the final report.

One reason for Dutch concern with information privacy is the fact that population registers were used by the Nazis during the Second World War to identify Jews. Another effect of the occupation, when identity cards were compulsory, is resistance to any new identity cards. Some of the concern has concentrated on proposals for a personal identification number (PIN). PINs already exist for most of the population, but they are only used for internal administrative purposes. In an opinion poll in 1985 60 per cent of those questioned did not object to having a PIN, but 47 per cent did not want PINs to be processed by computers. The government plans to introduce a system of two personal identifying numbers, one based on the PIN already being used internally, the other a 'fiscal' number to be used only for tax and social security purposes. This began in 1986, along with the introduction of a new data protection bill.[26]

Public opinion seems to be both concerned about information privacy and well informed. A 1979 survey reported that 57 per cent were in favour of a legal right to have information about themselves deleted from files, 51 per cent supported legislation on data protection (30 per cent knew that it was being considered), and 47 per cent were opposed to the use of PINs for the linkage of records.

As in France, there seems to have been much more public concern in the Netherlands about data protection than about general rights of public access to government information. The access to information law began with a draft bill included in the 1970 report of the Biesheuvel Commission, which was appointed in 1968 to consider government information. A modified version of that bill was adopted in 1978 and came into effect in 1980.

The access to information act apparently includes automated records, and applies to official documents held by central and provincial government. The right of access is not limited to Dutch citizens.[27] But the right of access to information is subject to a qualification which seems to be unique to the Netherlands: it is not a right to inspect and copy documents, but a right to information that may be provided by officials in the form of summaries of the contents of documents.

As in some other access regimes, the exemptions are in two classes: information which is completely exempt, and information exempt if the public interest in disclosure does not outweigh the interest given by law to the exemption. The absolute exemptions are for information which would harm national security or endanger the unity of the realm,[28] and for personal political opinions. Other exemptions are for information that would damage international relations, law enforcement, or the economic interests of the state.[29]

There is a specific exemption for information related to personal privacy, particularly medical and psychological information. This was criticized in the 1982 report of the evaluation commission as having been interpreted as a near-absolute exemption rather than a privacy interest to be weighed against others. It is in addition to a 'commercial privacy' exemption for information that would give an unfair advantage over third parties.[30] But there seems to be no equivalent to the Canadian 'third-party' procedure or the US 'reverse' Freedom of Information Act cases in which the interests of the requesting party and those of the third party can be heard and weighed.

The system of appeals under the Dutch act is to the Council of State, which has a quasi-judicial branch with the authority to examine documents containing the information requested. The law also requires a report to parliament on the functioning of the law. The first of these was due three years after the Act went into effect, and subsequent reports are due every five years.[31] To do this the government appointed an evaluation commission chaired by the same Mr Biesheuvel whose report inspired the legislation. The evaluation commission's first report was critical of the use of the privacy exemption, particularly in cases where the commission felt that it was used to withhold information about the official functions of a civil servant. Nevertheless, the commission did not propose that the exemption be changed in the law, but urged that the Council of State apply a balancing of interests test in cases where privacy is claimed as the basis for a refusal to disclose.

The Netherlands Data Protection Act became law on 1 July 1989. It applies to manual as well as computerized records, but does not apply to legal persons. It applies to both public and private sectors, but exempts personal data only processed for personal or domestic use. In a concession to press freedom and in recognition of the increasing automation of journalism, the law does not apply to data files intended solely for use in the supply of information by the press to the public. The police and security services are not subject to the Act, but are regulated by separate legislation. Codes of conduct are encouraged, and there are very few criminal penalties.

France

France has many specific privacy protection remedies, most of which were described in the 1972 study. The right to one's image, for example, has a direct counterpart in Prosser's American tort of the appropriation of one's likeness. The long-standing French statutory right to reply is steadily progressing towards an accepted international right, and most recently was included in the Council of Europe's recommended principles for direct broadcasting by satellite. A public opinion survey in 1975 found that financial and sexual privacy were considered the most important, and that social security and income tax authorities were thought to present the greatest threat to privacy in the public sector.[32]

France entered into data processing early and with enthusiasm, coining a new word, 'l'informatique', which includes more than just data processing, and perhaps more than 'informatics'. The French also quickly became aware of the threat to privacy and other liberties from the new technology. The Safari affair in 1974, in which the press reported an administrative plan to link all personal files with a personal identifier, aroused public concern. The Safari system was stopped, and a commission was set up by the Minister of Justice to consider measures to 'guarantee that the development of data processing in the public, semi-public, and private sectors would take place while respecting private life, individual liberties, and public liberties'.

The Commission came to be called after its chief rapporteur, Bernard Tricot, from the Conseil d'Etat. Its formal name was the 'Commission Nationale de l'Informatique et des Libertés' (CNIL), which was also the name given to the enforcement body recommended by the report. The report was delivered in 1975, and most of its recommendations were incorporated in the bill which became law in January 1978. This was followed by another law establishing a public right of access to administrative documents in July of that year, but this attracted far less attention than the data protection law.

The data protection law established five basic principles. The first was the establishment of the CNIL as an independent body with the job of advising on proposed data processing systems, monitoring existing systems, and doing research. The second was the establishment of a method of licensing or registration of data processing systems. The third was a general right of subject access and rectification. The fourth was the specific regulation of name-linked, or 'nominative', data. The fifth was simply that the CNIL's powers be successively phased in.

The debates over the bill in the National Assembly were largely over the composition and independence of the CNIL. It emerged as a body independent of government, with representatives of the National Assembly, Senate, Economic and Social Council, 'Conseil d'Etat', 'Cour de Cassation', and 'Cour des Comptes', along with data processing and other experts. But although the members of the CNIL come from these bodies, they are expressly bound not to take orders from them. The closest equivalent to the CNIL in independence is probably the *médiateur*, the French ombudsman.

The law itself covers both the public and private sectors, and has been interpreted as covering manual as well as automated files. Originally, the Tricot report recommended that legal as well as natural persons be protected. Corporations initially supported this as a measure which they could use against government, but then opposed it on realizing that rights of access could be used against them by their competitors. The government also decided against the idea, and the protection of legal persons was eventually dropped, leaving only an ambiguous reference that might refer to small firms.

The basic system of regulation is similar to that in most other European data protection statutes. Data processing systems which handle name-linked information must register, which most can do by a simplified form of declaration. The declaration includes information about interconnection with other systems, how long the information is retained, what security measures are taken, who has access to the information, and whether it will be sent to another country. The CNIL has wide powers of investigation and supervision, but violations of the law are reported to the public prosecutor.

The 'data subject rights' are essentially rights to be informed, and rights of access and correction. Under Article 27, when information is collected from data subjects they must be informed of their right of subject access, who will receive the information, and whether or not they are compelled to furnish the information. (Criminal investigations are exempt from these requirements.) There is an express prohibition on collecting information about racial origins, political, philosophical, or religious opinions, or trade union membership, without the express consent of the data subject. There is a modified exemption from this for the press.

Data subjects who want to know about files in general can consult the register maintained by the CNIL. This includes information about the lawful authority for particular public sector registers or date of declaration for most private sector registers, categories of information held, where access demands are to be sent, and any conditions imposed by the CNIL. There are, however, exemptions from these requirements for registers concerning state security, national defence, and public safety.[33] As mentioned before, individuals may also know of the existence of a register from the requirement that they be informed when the information is collected.

The right of subject access requires proof of identity and payment of a fee (20 francs in the public sector, 30 in the private). There is a further right to have errors corrected, and to have corrections communicated to any third parties who have received the incorrect information. Appeals may be made to the CNIL. There is no direct right of subject access to files related to national security, defence, or public safety. However, CNIL may designate a member (from the Conseil d'Etat, Cour de Cassation, or Cour des Comptes) to act on behalf of the data subject in examining such files.

A recent case illustrates the functioning of the CNIL in the use of information far from related to national security, and involving what most would regard as information of low sensitivity. The mayor of Grenoble had consulted the customer files of the local suppliers of electricity and gas because, he said, he wanted to welcome new residents. In an advisory opinion CNIL disapproved of the practice – just as a *Land* data protection commissioner in Germany had disapproved of a similar use.[34]

The French law on access to administrative documents was not the product of anything like the public pressure that there was for data protection, and it was not intended as a privacy protection measure. Rather, it was part of a series of administrative reforms which were perhaps influenced by foreign experience, as in the introduction of the *médiateur*. Like the data protection law, the general access law was preceded by a commission which also recommended that something very like itself should be established on a permanent basis with statutory authority.

This law is largely enforced by the supervision and recommendations of a body roughly equivalent to the CNIL, the 'Commission d'Accès aux Documents Administratifs' (CADA). The CADA has nine members, appointed from the national archives, parliament, the judiciary, the prime minister's office, and the universities. It may advise administrative departments at their request, and receives complaints from those who have been refused access. It does not have the power to order disclosure to be made, but only to make recommendations. The documents covered are, generally, all those under the control of government administrative bodies (but not judicial documents). It includes automatically processed data, although the overlap in jurisdiction with the CNIL has created some difficulties and been the subject of an agreement that is described below. Personal privacy considerations are built into the basic definitions of the law, with Article 1 providing a general right of access to 'non-nominative' documents, while Article 3 provides a right of access to 'nominative' documents. This right of subject access was initially limited to documents which were unfavourable to the data subject, but it was amended in 1979 (Article 6 *bis*) to cover any nominative documents. The law is not limited to French citizens, or even to natural persons, although restrictions have been imposed on foreign citizens.

In protecting personal privacy, the law seems to have two levels of protection: it first distinguishes between nominative and non-nominative documents, with the former only available to the person concerned; then, under Article 6, it includes 'private lives, personal, and medical files' in the eight general exemptions from the right of access to non-nominative documents. 'Nominative' is sometimes taken to mean name-linked, but the definition used is somewhat narrower. It is said by the CADA to be a document which contains an appreciation or a value judgement about an identified person.[35] Although there is no right of correction as such, there is a right to have observations added to an unfavourable judgement. Medical nominative documents are not available for direct subject access, but only through the intermediary of a doctor chosen by the subject. Such documents are limited to those containing information from the medical profession. Social welfare documents are available for direct subject access.[36]

Outside this there are other related administrative reforms which the right of subject access may trigger. One of these is the 1979 law which provides that reasons must be given for administrative decisions. A particular group which has made considerable use of the right of subject access has been civil servants. This right is, however, subject to all the general exemptions from access. There seems to be no procedure like that of the CNIL by which the CADA can exercise the right of subject access on behalf of a data subject to files which are exempt from access for reasons of national security or law enforcement. Also, there seems to be no third-party procedure by which someone whose privacy might be invaded by giving access to a file could be notified to consent or object to release. It may be that such a procedure will be introduced, not so much for reasons of privacy, but to aid in the application of the exemption for commercial and industrial secrets.[37]

One particular example may illustrate how the law has served to provide subject access to non-automated but important 'nominative' information: marked examination scripts. Before 1982 these were covered by the general exemption from access for secrets otherwise protected by law. After consultation with the CADA, the Ministry of Education ordered that examination papers be excluded from the list of other documents. So French baccalaureate students are now exercising their new right to examine their marked papers. Whether this has had any effect on the failure rate or on appeals is not yet clear.

The procedure followed is similar to that in most countries with access laws. If a request for a document is refused, the requester appeals to the CADA which, after appointing a rapporteur, asks for reasons from the department, and then writes an opinion (*avis*) which is given to the requester and the department. If disclosure is recommended but still not given, there is an appeal to an administrative judge. The route via the CADA is essential, and cannot be dispensed with.

The CADA has proposed an increase in its powers. It would like to be able to ask the Prime Minister to order a department to disclose documents, and it would like to be able, rather like the Canadian Information Commissioner, to appear in court.[38]

Both French laws seem to provide some rights to information privacy, and not only through the roughly parallel rights of subject access. The CNIL is specifically charged with supervising information practices with privacy protection in mind; this supervision includes both the public and the private sector, and is not necessarily limited to automated systems. The objective of CADA is administrative openness, but the basic distinction between nominative and non-nominative documents is a privacy protection measure, and the right to add an opinion to unfavourable judgements is another. (The initial limitation of subject access to unfavourable nominative documents suggests that a form of protection for information privacy was intended.)

The CADA pointed out in its first report that there were areas of possible conflict with the CNIL. An agreement was reached that, for non-nominative automated files, the CADA would concentrate on particular cases in which access was refused, while the CNIL would carry out general supervision. The CNIL would deal with nominative automated information, while non-nominative and non-automated records (that is, paper files not concerned with any particular person) would be dealt with exclusively by the CADA.

The question of jurisdiction has reached the Conseil d'Etat in a case about who should exercise the right of access to manual files of the national police. The Conseil d'Etat decided that access through the CADA was only possible if there was no possibility of access through the data protection law. The CNIL had the power to gain access through the appointment of a special rapporteur under Articles 34 and 35 of that law, so access to state security files, manual or automated, was to be exercised only through the CNIL.

New Zealand

The 1972 study did not cover New Zealand. It is included now for two reasons: it has the only data protection law in the world that is directed specifically, and only, towards regulating information about law enforcement, although that is almost certain to be replaced by general legislation; and it has followed Canada and Australia in adopting an access to government information law, even though this is probably the least effective of the three.

New Zealand privacy law is divided between common law principles (similar to those in England, but it has not yet followed the US example of developing a tort of invasion of privacy), the Human Rights Commission Act 1976, the Wanganvi Computer Centre Act 1976, and Part 4 of the Official Information Act 1982. The Bill of Rights adopted in 1990 did not include a right to privacy, but a data protection bill has been introduced and seems likely to become law.

The concern for privacy, as in many countries, arose when a census was held in 1971. A subcommittee of the Law Revision Commission began an inquiry into privacy and computers in the public and private sectors.[39] In the following year it was announced that a Law Enforcement Information System would be established, and that this would be able to exchange information with the Motor Vehicle Registry and Licence Holders System. The Government Statistician then announced that the statistics system would not be linked with the proposed law enforcement system.

A general election was called in 1972 and privacy became an issue, with a promise from Labour that legislation on the use of computerized personal data would be introduced. In the result, the Wanganui Computer Centre Act became law in September 1976. This authorized the establishment of the Centre, and created the office of Wanganvi Computer Centre Privacy Commissioner. The purpose of the Centre was to assist the Department of Justice, the Police Department, and the Ministry of Transport.

The detailed functions of the Centre were, for the Department of Justice, to compile inmate records and statistics, enforcement of fines and other court orders, case monitoring, and the processing of court documents. Ministry of Transport business included registration of motor vehicles and driving licences, traffic offences, and accident reports. Police Department records included firearms registration, wanted and missing persons, and lost or stolen property.

The Privacy Commissioner was given independence, being recommended by the House of Representatives (like the original Swedish ombudsman) for appointment by the government for a term of five years. His job is to receive and investigate complaints from anyone who 'has reason to believe that the information recorded about him on the computer system is wrongly so recorded because of inaccuracies, omissions, or the inclusion of unauthorized data, or is so recorded as to present a misleading impression'.[40]

The Commissioner has broad powers, although nothing is said about any authority to compel disclosures. Section 9 says that he

> may, from time to time, do all such things as are reasonably necessary to enable him to carry our his functions, including conducting, or

causing to be conducted, an inspection and audit of the Computer Centre and the computer system and their operations at any time.

He is doubly bound to secrecy about anything he learns. He and his staff are declared by section 12(1) to be subject to the Official Secrets Act (which, like its British model, makes it an offence to disclose any official information of any kind). Section 12(2) then directs that the Commissioner 'shall maintain secrecy in respect of all matters' concerning their work, and 12(3) says that any employee of the Commissioner must first take an oath 'that he will not divulge any information received by him under this Act except for the purposes of giving effect to this Act.' Section 10 describes the oath of secrecy to be taken by the Commissioner.

The Commissioner makes annual reports to Parliament, and he also reports on complaint investigations to the department concerned, with directions with which they must comply. If the Commissioner is not satisfied, he reports to the Prime Minister and to Parliament. The Act also provides a separate civil cause of action for disclosure of unauthorized or incorrect information from the computer system. Damages may be awarded for pecuniary loss, loss of benefit, or 'embarrassment, loss of dignity, and injury to ... feelings'. The right is in addition to any other cause of action, and the liability is strict ('It shall not be a defence ... that the breach was unintentional or without negligence'). The major limitation is that damages for injury to feelings are limited to NZ$500.[41]

Subject access in New Zealand is not entirely determined by the Commissioner. He can, on request and after identification, furnish copies of any information other than that described as *'modus operandi'* or 'wanted persons'. There is no charge, although only one request per person per year is allowed. However, the Commissioner may refuse a request if he decides that release would be 'detrimental to the interests of justice', although he may then inspect the records himself on behalf of the data subject. Perhaps most significant, in making such decisions he is subject to the directions of the Policy Committee of the Centre.

An additional privacy protection measure, though not one with any enforcement powers, was the creation of the Human Rights Commission and the incorporation of the International Covenants into New Zealand law by the Human Rights Commission Act of 1977. This has been followed by a Bill of Rights. The Human Rights Commission has the function of inquiring into any matter, in the public or private sector, which appears to infringe privacy. The Commission can report to the Prime Minister on any matter, to gather information, to invite representations, and to make public statements. The Commission does not have the power to investigate a particular complaint that an individual's privacy has been invaded, as distinct from a general inquiry. And the Commission is specifically barred from inquiring into the Wanganvi Computer Centre.

The Official Information Act 1982, like its counterparts in Australia and Canada, was not enacted primarily as a privacy protection measure, but to establish a system of more open government. As such, it would seem to be potentially less effective than the other two, if only because of its wide exemptions from disclosure and the nearly complete power of ministers to overrule recommendations from the ombudsman that documents be disclosed. As a privacy protection measure, however, it has some potential effectiveness, at least for personal data held in the public sector. It contains a separate section for personal information which resembles the US Privacy Act and the Canadian Privacy Act.

The Act's definition of 'official information' is 'any information held by ... a Department; or ... a Minister of the Crown in his official capacity; or ... an organisation'.[42] The exemptions are for library or museum material, information held 'solely as an agent or for the sole purpose of safe custody' for a body not subject to the Act, or evidence given to a Royal Commission.[43] 'Information' itself is not defined, however, leading one commentator to suggest that it is not limited to information recorded in a document.[44] His reasoning is based on a proposal made by the Danks Committee, which had drafted the original bill, that information should include 'not merely recorded data but knowledge of a fact or state of affairs by officers of the agency in their official capacity, e.g., when a particular report is to be presented'.[45] The definition of 'document' clearly does include automated information.[46]

The right of subject access is established by Part IV, which gives a right of access to 'personal information', defined as 'any official information held about an identifiable person'.[47] 'Person', for purposes of the Act, includes any citizen, permanent resident, or body incorporated in New Zealand.[48] But the definition of 'permanent resident' specifically excludes people who are either prohibited immigrants or who are obliged to 'leave New Zealand immediately or within a specified time.'[49] So the Official Information Act provides data protection of a sort, limited to the public sector but including both manual and automated records, for legal persons. The distinction between natural and legal persons is further acknowledged by the provision in section 24 that no fee is to be charged in the case of a request from a natural person.

The exemptions from the right of access are relatively broad. There is no right of access at all to personal information held by the Public Trustee or the Maori Trustee when they act in a fiduciary capacity.[50] The law enforcement exemptions include one against disclosure of information which might prejudice 'the maintenance of the law', and another for information about a person detained or convicted of an offence if the information would be likely to prejudge or prejudice that person's rehabilitation or endanger the safety of another person.[51] Disclosure to anyone under 16 may be refused if it would be 'contrary to that person's interests', and medical information may be refused to anyone if disclosure would be 'likely to prejudice the physical or mental health of that person' (although this decision requires consultation with the person's doctor).[52] Another exemption, which is common to most access to government information laws, is for information protected by legal professional privilege.[53] One exemption for information which might be considered to be in the interests of the privacy of third parties, but which is potentially much wider than that, is if disclosure 'would breach an expressed or implied promise' made to a person that information 'would be held in confidence'.[54] (This section was the one most used to refuse requests for personal information during the first six months of the Act.[55]) The exemption to protect the privacy of others is in section 27(1)(b), which exempts information from disclosure if it 'would involve the unwarranted disclosure of the affairs of another person'. If this is to be read together with the general exemptions under the Act, it would seem to recognize the privacy of the dead, as section 9 includes, in the 'other reasons' to justify withholding information, the protection of the privacy of individuals (both alive and deceased).

If the request for access is granted, the applicant can seek that corrections be made, or, failing that, a notation attached indicating the nature of the correction requested but not made.[56] There is a legal duty to inform the applicant of the action taken, but the only statutory recourse if a request is refused is by a complaint to the ombudsman.[57] The ombudsman's powers are to investigate and recommend, but there are important differences which depend on the kind of information being sought. The ombudsman can investigate complaints about the refusal of a request for access to specified information which does not relate to a particular person under Part II of the Act. This, however, is subject to a possible 'super veto' by the Prime Minister, who can certify that disclosure would prejudice the nation's security, defence, or international relations, and the Attorney-General has a similar power to certify that disclosure would prejudice the prevention, investigation, or detection of offences.[58] If such a certificate is issued the ombudsman is barred from making a recommendation that disclosure may be made, although he may recommend that it be given further consideration. If there is no such certificate, the ombudsman's recommendation becomes a legal duty to disclose if the responsible minister does not object in writing within 21 days.[59] During the first six months that the Act was in operation there were four such ministerial vetoes, one of which could be said to be in the interest of privacy. The first use of the veto was by the Minister of Justice and the Postmaster-General to stop the release of an alphabetical list of voters.[60]

The ombudsman's powers when a request for personal information (under Part IV) is refused are between the two extremes described above. After investigation, the ombudsman makes recommendation to the responsible minister. If after a 'reasonable time' no action is taken, the ombudsman 'may send a copy of the report and recommendations to the Prime Minister, and may therefore make such report to Parliament on the matter as he thinks fit'.[61]

The Act also established a three-person Information Authority to monitor the operation of the law. It was first chaired by Sir Alan Danks, who chaired the committee which recommended the Act. The Authority has no enforcement power. It is not permitted to inquire into any investigation conducted by the ombudsman, nor, like the Human Rights Commission, may it inquire into the operation of the Wanganvi Computer Centre.[62]

The Act does not contemplate any resolution of disputes over access by the courts, and bars any application for judicial review until a complaint 'is determined'.[63] However, it seems at least possible that some decisions under the Act may be subject to judicial review, and some lawyers in New Zealand intend to apply for this remedy.[64]

New Zealand published a data protection bill in 1990, which was passed in 1990. The Act is scheduled to become law in two stages in 1991 and 1992. The first stage provides for a Privacy Commissioner to oversee data-matching programmes. The second stage gives rights of subject access, although the Human Rights Commission is empowered to grant exemptions from the Act's principles in the public and private sector. The second stage has repealed the Wanganvi Computer Centre Act.

Canada

Canada's Protection of Privacy Act 1973 was limited to the regulation of telephone-tapping and electronic surveillance, and will be discussed later. At the provincial level there are three statutes[65] creating torts of intentional invasion of privacy. Courts in Quebec have interpreted the civil law doctrine of *actio injuriarum* as establishing a right to privacy. Courts in other provinces approach the subject in the traditional common law way of enforcing particular remedies rather than applying a general doctrine.[66] At the federal level, Canada legislated to protect information privacy in Part IV of the Canadian Human Rights Act of 1977. The substance of that law was rather like the US Privacy Act of

1974: it covered information on natural persons held by the federal government, not distinguishing between manual and automated systems, and established basic principles of relevance, accuracy and fairness. In procedure, however, it more resembled European legislation in creating the post of Privacy Commissioner to hear complaints.

In 1982 Canada again acted on privacy, but was the first country (and the only, thus far) to adopt a single legislative package for both access to government information and privacy protection. As in the United States, this had been preceded by legislation at the provincial level, particularly on access to government information. The Privacy Act is not really a data protection act in the European sense: like the US Act of the same name, it does not regulate information handling in the private sector at all. The Access to Information Act is an interesting combination of US and Scandinavian features, with some modifications for a common law country with a Westminster-model constitution.

The Privacy Act extends the subject access rights of the 1977 Human Rights Act, which were limited to information used in taking decisions about the person concerned. The 1982 Act applies to both manual and automated information under the control of the federal government. Apart from the subject access right, the Act provides a set of principles governing the collection and processing of personal information by government departments.[67] These are very similar to the basic principles of data protection, including provisions that the information should be accurate and up to date, that it should not be used for a purpose inconsistent with the purpose for which it was collected, that the individual concerned should be informed about the purpose of information collection unless it would defeat the purpose of collection, and that information should not be disclosed without the consent of the person concerned, unless it satisfies one of 12 conditions. There is also a more general authorization to disclose personal information if it would clearly benefit the individual concerned or if the public interest in disclosure would clearly outweigh the privacy interest; in such a case, notice must be given to the Privacy Commissioner, who acts to protect the privacy interest, and may notify the individual concerned.

One provision to assist those who want to exercise their rights under the Privacy Act is a personal information index published annually, listing all government personal information banks, together with considerable information about what is held and whether exemption from subject access is claimed.[68] The right of subject access, like the general right of access to official information, is limited to Canadian citizens and permanent residents.

Most of the exemptions from access under the Privacy Act are identical to those under the Access to Information Act, but some are drafted for the special circumstances of subject access. For example, access to medical information about the requestor may be refused in the best interests of that person, as defined in regulations (very similar to the compromise adopted under the British Data Protection Act). Those sentenced for criminal offences may be refused access to information about themselves if the institutional programme or supervision would be seriously disrupted. Access to information about security clearances may be refused if it would lead to the identification of confidential informants. There is also a power of the government to designate information banks as exempt if they predominantly contain information relating to international affairs and defence or law enforcement.

In addition to the right of subject access, there is a right of correction. This includes a right to have a notation circulated to others if disclosure to them was made for administrative purposes within two years of the correction. The procedure for complaints to the Privacy Commissioner, investigations, and procedures for appeal to the courts are almost identical to those in the Access to Information Act. There is one significant exception, however.

The Privacy Act has no 'third-party procedure' by which the competing interests of the data subject in securing access, and those of a third party with a privacy interest against disclosure, may be resolved. This may be explained in part by the provisions of section 8 of the Privacy Act, which says that requests for information concerning individuals may be released for one of 12 relatively narrow purposes, or with the consent of the person concerned. The difficulty is with the general power to disclose information if the public interest in disclosure clearly outweighs the privacy interest of the person concerned. In such a case there is no duty to notify the person concerned, only to notify the Privacy Commissioner, who then acts to protect the privacy interest, and may, but is not required to, notify the subject. This may well have been because of difficulties in tracing individuals, and serves to emphasize the need in some circumstances for some authority to act on behalf of those whose privacy may be threatened without their knowledge. But it seems somewhat anomalous that the prospect of financial harm resulting from a contemplated disclosure would apparently require actual notice to the person concerned under the Access to Information Act while the prospect of possible emotional distress would not.

The primary purpose of the Access to Information Act is not the protection of personal privacy, particularly as it was adopted with the companion Privacy Act. However, the general right of access to government records can be used for the purpose of subject access. One of the purposes of passing both laws together was to avoid the sort of overlap and conflict under the US laws, and they are drafted to be as consistent as possible.

The basic right of access may be exercised by any Canadian citizen or permanent resident.[69] The right applies to any 'record' under the control of any federal government institution, and the definition clearly includes computer-stored information.[70] (One interesting feature of the Act is that, although it is not as completely retrospective as the US equivalent, it does have what may be called partial phased retrospection, by which it was easier to refuse access to documents more than five years old during the first two years following enactment.) The exemptions fall into two general categories: mandatory and permissive, according to the discretion which the government institution has to grant access. The definition of the exemptions also involves a class or injury test. These are very similar to tests established in the law of 'public interest immunity' (formerly Crown privilege), concerning the possible immunity of some kinds of evidence from pre-trial discovery. The class test is satisfied by a mere showing that the requested document is in an exempted category. The injury test requires some proof that the injury specified would be caused by disclosure.

The exemptions are more detailed than those in the US Act, and those connected with law enforcement are most likely to be encountered by individuals seeking access to records concerning themselves. Some of the other exemptions might sometimes prevent subject access, however. The institution must refuse access to information obtained in confidence from any other national government, international organization, or province; access may be allowed only with the consent of those who provided the information or if it has already been made public.[71] Access may be refused if disclosure is reasonably likely to be injurious to federal or provincial affairs, to international relations, to national defence, or to anti-subversive measures.[72]

Access to information may be refused if the information was obtained by an investigative body during investigations into crime, if it relates to law enforcement techniques, if its disclosure would be detrimental to the security of a penal institution, or if it could reasonably be expected to facilitate the commission of an offence.[73] One law enforcement exemption, for information obtained by the Royal Canadian Mounted Police while acting for a province or municipality, requires explanation: the RCMP, although Canada's federal police force, also acts as the police for some of the provinces.[74]

The Canadian Act has fairly detailed provisions which exempt information from disclosure in the interests of personal privacy, as well as a procedure which seems more detailed than those of any other country. One of these exemptions might apply to some law enforcement information (from informers) and some family information (to potentially violent spouses, for example): it exempts information if disclosure might reasonably be expected to threaten the safety of individuals.[75] Another, which is common to most access laws, is for information subject to lawyer–client privilege.[76]

It is the general exemption for information affecting the privacy of a third party, and the procedure for resolving disputes, that is potentially the most interesting. There are actually two types of third-party privacy interests: financial, and general. The financial privacy interest is part of a more general provision exempting information about trade secrets, or financial, commercial, scientific, or technical information which has consistently been treated as confidential. There is also an exemption if disclosure of the information would cause financial loss, prejudice the competitive position, or interfere with the negotiations of a third party.[77] There is, however, authority to give access if the public interest in disclosure outweighs that of the third party concerned.

The procedure to be followed in such cases is complex in its details, but simple in design. It provides that if a request for access is received which involves third-party interests, the third parties concerned must be notified and given an opportunity to argue against disclosure (or to consent) before access is granted. This was introduced largely to avoid the experience of the United States, which has no such procedure in its law, and which has been faced with a plethora of 'reverse' Freedom of Information lawsuits attempting to restrain disclosures. All the American cases, as well as the few under the Canadian procedure, have involved third-party commercial interests, but they could equally be used to invoke personal privacy interests. The procedure provides various time-limits for notice and counternotice, all of which, if used to the maximum but with no extensions, take 100 days. One of the curiosities of the procedure, and it is not clear whether it is deliberate, is that it is possible for third-party cases to go directly to court without involving the Information Commissioner, as did the first reported case under the Act.

The more general personal privacy exemption in section 19 of the Access to Information Act refers to section 3 of the Privacy Act for the kinds of personal information that should not generally be released. This is not absolute, and information about the title and responsibilities of a government employee may be released. There is also a provision which touches on the question of whether a right to information privacy survives death: information about those dead more than 20 years may be disclosed.

The office of Information Commissioner is very like that of the JO in Sweden with reponsibility for Freedom of the Press Act complaints. The Commissioner is appointed with Parliamentary approval for a term of seven years, with a possible reappointment for another seven.[78] With Assistant Commissioners and staff, the Commissioner's job is to investigate complaints, take part in judicial review, and report to Parliament.

Complaints may be on almost any aspect of access to information, including the language used, but most complaints are likely to be about refusals to grant access. They must be submitted in writing within one year. The Commissioner may, however, begin investigations without receiving a complaint. Although the Commissioner has extensive powers of investigation and immunity, there is no power to order disclosure, only to recommend. The Commissioner may, however, go to court on behalf of the person seeking access or as a party, with leave of the court. The court has broad powers to hold hearings *in camera* and to consider *ex parte* applications to reduce to a minimum the classic problem of secrecy and privacy litigation: how to decide between competing claims for disclosure and secrecy without making the disclosure. The burden of proof is on the government institution, and the court can order disclosure.

How have these two carefully drafted laws, drawing on experience around the world, worked? Of the actions under the Access Act, only a few involved questions of personal privacy. (If legal persons were considered to have privacy rights, however, all the third-party corporate cases would be included.) One particular case illustrates some of the problems. The application of a Canadian citizen to bring his wife from a foreign country was rejected, on the ground that her previous marriage in that country made her marriage to the Canadian invalid. The wife's request for access under the Privacy Act was denied because she was not a Canadian citizen or resident. The husband then asked for information about the rejection of his sponsorship, and was refused because it was personal information about another person. Finally, the husband's lawyer applied for access with a consent to disclosure signed by the wife. The department refused, saying that the statute said that it 'may' disclose personal information with the consent of the subject, with the implication that it also 'may not'. At that point the Information Commissioner applied for judicial review.

Another case with privacy implications started with a journalist's request for the information about the salaries paid to 13 government appointees. This was refused on the ground that it was personal information, and that, although the Access Act allows disclosure of salary ranges, the salaries concerned were precise rather than ranges. Eight days before the case was to begin in court, the Prime Minister released some of the information.

The cases brought to court under the Privacy Act are less revealing. In one case, *Reyes* v. *Secretary of State*, a Chilean refugee whose citizenship application had been refused asked for access to personal information and was refused again. The reasons given were that disclosure would endanger defence, international relations, or counter-subversion efforts. Later another reason, that disclosure would

injure a law enforcement investigation, was added. The Privacy Commissioner agreed. After an *in camera* court hearing, in which the
complainant's lawyer was not allowed to see the documents, the
judge concluded that the exemptions had been applied correctly.

The reports of decisions by the Privacy Commissioner which have
not reached, and may not reach, the courts give a more balanced
picture of how the Act is working. A complex complaint about an
attempt by Revenue Canada to cross-match records with those in the
city data banks of Kitchener, Ontario, was largely rejected. In part
this was because only Revenue Canada was subject to the Act, but
also because 'it is ominous and threatening only top potential tax
evaders'.[79] A complaint that the confidentiality of the pay and de-
ductions of some lower-paid civil servants was breached by the
manual distribution of pay cheques was upheld. The Commissioner
called the open distribution of pay cheques 'invitations to privacy
violations', adding that giving senior officials cheques in envelopes
was 'perhaps more indefensible.' 'The story of how each federal
government pay cheque now has (or is about to have) its own envel-
ope is a testimonial to privacy enlightenment at the Treasury Board
and a model of systematic privacy protection.'[80]

Another case illustrates how privacy interests can compete. A
woman complained to a government department about the political
activities of a civil servant while on sick leave. The report does not
say whether she was told that her identity or the substance of the
complaint would be kept confidential, although she clearly expected
her identity not to be disclosed to the employee. He was told who
had complained about him, and he talked about it to the press. The
woman's complaint to the Commissioner that her privacy had been
invaded by the disclosure of her identity was rejected, with the comment that there is 'a greater danger in not giving such information to
the person concerned as individuals could become the victims of
unknown and malicious accusations. A difficult trade-off has been
made and the public should be aware of that trade-off.'[81]

A man whose rural mail delivery contract was not renewed complained about the refusal to allow access to several pages in his
personnel record. Several of them were letters from residents on his
route complaining about 'mail in the wrong boxes, obscene language,
and garbage in mail boxes'. After intervention by the Commissioner,
Canada Post agreed to release some of the letters, omitting the
writers' names and addresses out of concern that the complainant
would retaliate.[82]

According to the 1984–5 Annual Report, 369 completed complaints
had been processed. Of those, 140 were justified, 219 dismissed, and
ten abandoned. The greatest number of complaints (94) were about
Correctional Service Canada, perhaps suggesting that the privacy of

prisoners is one of the more important particular issues. There were 55 complaints about National Defence, almost all of which had to do with access to performance evaluation forms. Next were the Royal Canadian Mounted Police (48), Employment and Immigration (40), and the Parole Board (25).[83]

It is perhaps worth noting that, in the interests of privacy, complaints are handled confidentially by both Commissioners. This is certainly allowed, and probably required, by the Acts. But it raises a related question when compared with the relatively open procedure in court, at least so far as the complainant is concerned. Administrative procedures generally provide less publicity, or more privacy, for the settlement of disputes than do judicial procedures. The issues involved in the conflict between personal privacy and open justice are not particularly affected by technology, except in the sense that newspaper reports are now more easily searched, but the Canadian Act illustrates one aspect of the issue, and at least raises the question of whether the greater publicity of judicial review might deter some from exercising their rights under the Acts.

The Canadian legislation is an improvement on US law in its coherence at least; its effectiveness in promoting transparence and protecting privacy will depend on the interpretations of the Commissioners and the courts. But the Canadian Privacy Act does not attempt to protect privacy in the private sector, and it is unlikely that it meets the standards of the Council of Europe Convention. In June 1984, however, Canada announced its decision to adhere to the OECD Guidelines, committing itself 'to encourage private sector corporations to develop voluntary privacy protection codes'.

Canada legislated at the federal level in 1973 to control surveillance by telephone interceptions and electronic devices. The Protection of Privacy Act 1973 makes both criminal offences unless committed under a judicial warrant.[84] Evidence obtained by such methods without a warrant is inadmissible, and punitive damages may be awarded.[85]

United States of America

The United States probably produces more privacy case law than any other common law jurisdiction. The 1972 ICJ report suggested two strains in American life relevant to privacy, 'namely a strongly assertive competitiveness and, partly as a result of religious influences, an opposing tendency to give protection against interference with the sacred rights of the individual'.[86] It is possible to identify other strains in American thinking, some of which may help to explain why the USA has followed rather different lines of development in privacy law in recent years.

One particular aspect of the American urge to compete is litigious-
ness. Whether the relatively high proportion of lawyers in the population is the result or cause of this is difficult to say, but De Tocqueville
noticed the tendency of Americans to resolve most issues, including
political ones, into legal disputes. It is also possible that the contin-
gency fee system, by which an attorney acquires a financial interest
in the outcome of a case, may be an influence. Whatever the cause,
there is no shortage of lawyers prepared to argue that the law should
be extended to provide new remedies. The courts are relatively receptive to novel legal arguments, and the federal system provides
judicial as well as legislative laboratories where new rights may be
created, tested, and then perhaps copied.

Prosser's four torts were the product of judicial creativity, and
state privacy statutes such as the one in New York provide varying
levels of legislative protection. At the federal level the power of the
Supreme Court to strike down state or federal statutes if they are
found to be unconstitutional is particularly important in asserting
fundamental individual rights such as the right to privacy. It is also
important that the Supreme Court can articulate developing rights
such as privacy, which was found in the penumbra of other specified
rights such as freedom of speech and protection against unreasonable search and seizure.

The development of privacy law in the USA has thus proceeded at
two judicial levels: the common law level by which judges fashion
remedies for particular invasions of privacy, and the constitutional
level at which the federal courts measure statutes against the constitutional right to privacy. There is a very large body of American
literature about both types of development. The single most important judicial decision in privacy law since *Griswold* v. *Connecticut*[87] is
probably the abortion ruling in *Roe* v. *Wade*,[88] which has already been
considered.

The federal legislature has also played an important part in the
development of privacy protection law, particularly in the area of
informational privacy. Apart from Finland, the United States was the
first country to enact a national access to government information
law (in 1966) after Sweden. As in Sweden, the Freedom of Information Act was not intended primarily as a privacy protection measure.
It was primarily a reform of administrative law in form, and was
largely intended as an aid to general public scrutiny of the federal
executive.

The Act provides a general public right of access to federal government records, subject to nine general exemptions, with appeals to the
ordinary federal courts. The exemption most relevant to personal
privacy is the one for 'personnel and medical files the disclosure of
which would constitute a clearly unwarranted invasion of personal

privacy'. In the early days of the Act, after it went into effect in 1967, there were bureaucratic attempts at refusing requests for access to records made by the people concerned on the ground that disclosure would be an unwarranted invasion of their privacy. This practice was never tested in court, and stopped after a 'conference committee' from both houses of Congress made it clear that protection of privacy was not intended to justify such refusal of what would now be called 'subject access'.

During the political upheavals of the late 1960s increasing use was made of the Freedom of Information Act by individuals to ask for files compiled on them by the federal security agencies. The climate of distrust of government resulting from the complex of events now known as Watergate made two major legislative changes possible: the first was the passage of the 1974 amendments to the Freedom of Information Act which strengthened it; the second was the passage of the Privacy Act in the same year. So far as subject access to records is concerned, the two statutes overlap. Both apply only to records held by the federal executive, and do not regulate the private sector. Both apply to manual and automated records. The Freedom of Information Act is slightly broader in its application to law enforcement agencies, while the Privacy Act has a near-blanket exemption for the Central Intelligence Agency and the Federal Bureau of Investigation. But the Privacy Act includes rights of deletion and correction which are not available under the Freedom of Information Act. It is not yet entirely clear which Act prevails if there is a conflict between them, but agencies will usually disclose records if they are disclosable under either law. There are also differences in the permitted procedures: the Privacy Act apparently allows agencies to make regulations for the disclosure of medical information only through a designated doctor.[89]

Before turning in more detail to the operation of these and other statutes, it is perhaps worth noting that both these laws provided rights against the federal government only, and that the rights were unaccompanied by any enforcement agency. These may illustrate two further strains in American life with implications for privacy law. One is a deep-rooted suspicion of governmental agencies in general and federal government in particular. A consequence is that it was easier for Congress to provide rights of subject access against the federal bureaucracy than it would have been to provide a similar general right of subject access in the private sector. A second strain, closely related to the first, is a preference for legal rights to be protected by self-help rather than an administrative agency. These are not necessarily particular to any place on the political spectrum. Although the creation of regulatory agencies at the federal level was part of the Roosevelt New Deal, there is now considerable suspicion of such agencies in liberal circles on the ground that they become 'captives' of the industries they were created to regulate.

For these reasons it seems very unlikely that the United States will legislate in the manner of most countries which have signed the Council of Europe Data Protection Convention, creating a supervisory body with broad registration and enforcement powers over those in both the public and private sector who engage in the automatic processing of personal data. Even with a major shift in political orientation at the federal level it is unlikely that privacy legislation would go further than a version of the Canadian Act, providing some sort of privacy protection officer to regulate the federal government. Some implications of this for possible restrictions on transborder data flows will be considered later.

The Freedom of Information Act is a privacy protection measure in two senses: it provides a right of subject access to records, both manual and automated, held by the federal government; and it protects the privacy of third parties by exempting records from access if disclosure would involve a 'clearly unwarranted invasion of privacy'. This is the only one of the nine general exemptions from the rule of disclosure which involves a balancing of interests test: the court first considers whether disclosure would involve an invasion of privacy at all; if it would, then the court considers the purpose of the requested disclosure to see if it justifies the invasion of privacy. It is thus an exception to the principle of the Act that the right of access is not based on a demonstration of a 'need to know'. Two cases illustrate how the exemption works. In *Getman* v. *National Labor Relations Board*[90] academic researchers wanted disclosure of the names of union members who had voted in an NLRB-supervised ballot so that a questionnaire could be sent to them. The court considered that an invasion of privacy was involved, but that the purpose of the request justified it. But in *Wine Hobby* v. *Internal Revenue Service*[91] the sellers of home wine-making kits were refused access to the names and address of people who had registered with the tax authorities, as those who make wine at home are required to do by law. An invasion of privacy would be involved, and the commercial purpose of the request did not justify it.

Although this discussion is concerned with the protection of personal privacy, some explanation of the Act's exemption from disclosure for 'trade secrets' is relevant. The exemption for 'trade secrets and commercial or financial information obtained from a person and privileged or confidential' comes close to providing a measure of protection for the privacy of legal persons. It is a difficult exemption to interpret, quite apart from the initial difficulty in unravelling its grammar, and it has given rise to the 'reverse FOIA' actions which are the US equivalent of (and perhaps the inspiration for) the statutory Canadian third-party procedure. In such actions a corporate party who feels that a decision by a federal agency to disclose information obtained from the corporation should not be carried out may ask a federal court to stop the disclosure. The possibilities of such actions were limited somewhat in 1980 by the Supreme Court decision in the *Chrysler* case, in which the Court refused to stop the requested disclosure by the Department of Defense of information about employment of minorities which Chrysler had provided to the Department.

Although such third-party actions thus far have been limited to corporate information, it seems at least possible that similar action might be taken to oppose the disclosure of personal information. The difficulty is that there is no requirement in the Act for those whose privacy might be invaded by disclosure to be notified. The decision is for the department that has received a request for disclosure, and only comes before the courts if the department refuses and the party seeking disclosure appeals. Quite apart from the absence of any notification requirement, the Act is less than satisfactory in providing opportunities for third parties to protect their privacy interests. There is no review mechanism between the final administrative decision and an appeal to the courts. Individuals who learned of a proposed disclosure of information concerning them might be reluctant to go to court, if only for financial reasons. Litigants in the USA generally pay their own legal expenses, regardless of who wins. The important exception to this rule in the Freedom of Information Act provides that someone whose request for information has 'substantially prevailed' over the government's refusal may have legal expenses paid by the government. That provision is very unlikely to cover an individual opposing disclosure of information by the government. At the very least, this possibility seems to be an argument for a Canadian-style privacy commissioner who might take action to defend the privacy interests of those unable to do so themselves (or perhaps not capable of being traced and notified).

There is one other exemption to the Freedom of Information Act which also serves to protect personal privacy: the exemption from disclosure of any information exempted by another statute. This was used initially as a wide exemption by some agencies which relied on pre-FOIA laws giving them wide discretion to disclose or not. After the Supreme Court decision in *Robertson* v. *Federal Aviation Administration* the Act was amended so that information is exempted from disclosure by another statute only if the other law 'requires that the matter be withheld from the public in such manner as to leave no discretion on the issue, or establishes particular criteria for withholding or refers to particular types of matter to be withheld'. The main effect of this exemption now is to protect from disclosure records such as tax returns and census information.

The right of 'subject access' under the Freedom of Information Act is not absolute, and it is even more limited under the Privacy Act (although perhaps compensated for by that Act's rights of correction and deletion). The major limits in both laws on the right of subject access are those of national security and law enforcement. The exemption in the FOIA for national security is for documents 'properly' classified in the interests of national security. This means that the courts have the power to examine the documents *in camera* and decide whether the classification was justified or not. The courts have exercised this ability to overrule executive classification sparingly in such national security cases. However, people subject to false derogatory information have succeeded in obtaining access to their records. One illustrative case is that of Professor Penn Kimball, of Columbia University, who found that Federal Bureau of Investigation informants had labelled him as a security risk in the 1940s. Although he had a successful journalistic and academic career, he was turned down for several government posts without knowing the reason until he filed a Freedom of Information request in the 1970s.[92]

The exemption for reasons of law enforcement was originally broadly worded and broadly interpreted, but it was narrowed considerably by the 1974 amendments. To the extent that the exemption now allows the refusal of subject access on the grounds that it would, among other things, 'interfere with enforcement proceedings ... disclose investigative techniques and procedures, or ... endanger the life or physical safety of law enforcement personnel', the exemption reduces the effect of subject access to protect personal privacy. There are, of course, legitimate law enforcement interests that should in some cases prevail over the right of subject access. The difficulty with the Freedom of Information Act is that there is no intermediate procedure between disclosure to the data subject and secrecy. An independent privacy commissioner who could examine records on behalf of the data subject might serve to protect privacy without prejudicing law enforcement.

The law enforcement exemption does protect privacy interests in two rather narrow ways. One is the exemption of records that would 'disclose the identity of a confidential source and, in the case of a record compiled by a criminal law enforcement authority in the course of a criminal investigation, or by an agency conducting a lawful national security intelligence investigation, confidential information furnished only by the confidential source'. The other is a near-repetition of the general privacy exemption which exempts investigatory records compiled for law enforcement purposes to the extent that disclosure would 'constitute an unwarranted invasion of personal privacy'. It has been said judicially that the absence of 'clearly' from this exemption provides broader protection for privacy than in the general exemption.[93]

The Privacy Act of 1974 also provides a subject access right similar to that under the Freedom of Information Act, and this is an appropriate place to compare the two provisions before considering the information practice rules established by the Privacy Act. The right of access under the Freedom of Information Act extends to everyone, while the equivalent Privacy Act right is limited to 'a citizen of the United States or an alien lawfully admitted for permanent residence'.[94] The exemptions from the right of subject access in the Privacy Act are almost always far broader than those in the Freedom of Information Act. For example, general exemptions are provided in the Privacy Act to cover any records maintained by the Central Intelligence Agency and most records maintained by the Federal Bureau of Investigation or other federal law enforcement body, including the office which considers applications for pardons. However, there is a right to request amendment of a record on the ground that the information is not 'accurate, relevant, timely, or complete'. If the agency refuses to make the requested correction, it may be appealed to the courts. If the appeal fails, the data subject still has a right to file a 'concise statement setting forth the reasons for his disagreement with the refusal of the agency'.

There is another right under the Privacy Act for compensation if the data subject suffers harm from a failure of an agency to maintain records which are 'accurate, relevant, timely, or complete'. Unlike the other rights of access and correction, this right requires some proof of an adverse effect of the erroneous information. Also, the data subject must show that the agency's action was 'intentional or willful' in order to recover damages.

Apart from the rights of subject access, correction, and damages the Act limits personal information-gathering by federal agencies and requires them to inform the public about the types of personal information which they process. It applies to 'systems of records', which is defined as a collection of information about an individual that contains his name or other identifying particular. (It should perhaps be noted that the Act is assumed to apply only to natural persons. However, there is a division in judicial authority as to whether the law applies equally to 'individuals acting in personal capacity and individuals acting in an entrepreneurial capacity'.[95])

The agencies are bound to collect only that personal information that is relevant and necessary for their statutory purposes, and they are required to publish notices at least every year of the records maintained, together with information about how to exercise the right of subject access. Like many data protection acts, the law requires that individuals from whom personal information is being sought be told the agency's statutory authority, the purpose of the collection, whether providing the information is voluntary or mandatory, and the consequences of refusal.

The agencies are also bound not to disclose personal information further, although this is subject to 11 rather broad exceptions. The most important of these is probably the one allowing disclosure for a 'routine use' compatible with the purpose for which the information was collected. Another exception includes disclosures required in response to requests under the Freedom of Information Act. (This is not quite the threat to privacy that it might seem at first: refusals of requests for personal information under the FOIA can be justified under the privacy exemption, and agency discretionary disclosures are not 'required'.) Perhaps as important as the fairly flexible rule against further disclosures of personal information is the requirement that agencies keep a record of such disclosures. The records need not be kept for intra-agency disclosures or any made under the Freedom of Information Act. But other disclosures must be recorded with the date and purpose of the disclosure, and the name and address of the recipient. The records must be kept for five years or the life of the record, whichever is longer. Disclosures made for the purposes of law enforcement investigations must be recorded, but they need not be disclosed to the subject on request; the record of all other disclosures becomes part of the file subject to the general rules on subject access.

The Privacy Act was the product of compromise, heavily influenced by the political mood in Washington in 1974. It, and the strengthening amendments to the Freedom of Information Act, would almost certainly not have become law had it not been for the revelations surrounding Watergate. One result of the compromise was that the Federal Privacy Board, which the Senate had proposed to have broad powers over both the public and private sectors, did not come into existence. Another result was the establishment of a temporary Privacy Protection Study Commission, which issued a report in 1977 entitled *Privacy in an Information Society*. In it the Commission restated the 'eight privacy commandments' of openness, individual access, correction and amendment, collection limitation, internal use limitation, disclosure limitation, information management, and accountability. These have been incorporated into a number of bills, few of which have become law. Regulation of the private sector is directed at particular practices and industries, through legislation such as the Fair Credit Reporting Act 1970, the Fair Credit Billing Act 1974 (amended in 1976), the Family Educational Rights and Privacy Act 1976, the Equal Credit Opportunity Act 1974 (amended 1976), the Fair Debt Collection Practices Act 1977, the Right to Financial Privacy Act 1978, and the Computer Matching and Privacy Protection Act 1988.

Pressure for regulation of the private sector was increased in 1991 by a plan to sell *Lotus Marketplace*, a product of names, addresses, and marketing information on 120 million consumers on CD-ROM disks. The product was dropped after heavy criticism. A Data Protection Bill to create a permanent, but non-regulatory Data Protection Board was introduced in 1990 and again in 1991, but seems unlikely to succeed. Although general data protection legislation regulating the public sector does not seem likely, sectoral regulatory statutes are frequently adopted at the state and federal level. Pressure for legislation is increasing from Europe. The European Community's draft directive has attracted attention and criticism, and the British Data Protection Registrar's order prohibiting transfer of personal data to the United States because of inadequate protection is the first measure to have concrete effect, although in a very minor case.[96]

Australia

Australia is a federal state, like Canada, the USA, Germany, and Austria. However, it has no real equivalent to the guarantees of basic rights as those countries do, either in their original basic law, like the US Bill of Rights, or by incorporation of the European Convention, or both. The courts have been nearly as reluctant as English courts to recognize a general right to privacy. In 1937 the High Court (the country's highest federal court of appeal) refused any remedy to a racetrack owner who complained that races were not only being observed from a platform on neighbouring land, but that a commentary on them was being broadcast.[97]

As a 1979 Law Reform Commission report on 'Privacy Sanctions and Remedies' pointed out: 'It is important to note, at the outset, that there is no general right to privacy conferred by the Australian Constitution. In this regard, the position can be contrasted with that which has developed in the United States.' Australia's privacy protection laws are thus much like those in the United Kingdom, supplemented by particular statutes at the federal and state level.

At the federal level, Australia has paid considerable attention to the study of privacy issues. The Labor government elected in 1973 had promised 'the right to privacy to be protected by Commonwealth and State laws'. This was followed by a study of privacy law by the standing committee of Commonwealth and State Attorneys-General.

The Law Reform Commission, established in 1973, was given a reference in 1976 to 'enquire into and report upon undue intrusions into and interferences with privacy', and to propose 'legislative or other measures that are required to provide proper protection and redress for privacy invasion in the Commonwealth's sphere', as well as proposals for changes in Territorial law. Particular attention was to be paid to data storage systems. The Commission published three papers in 1979 and 1980 proposing specific remedies for publication of 'sensitive private facts', surreptitious surveillance of the home, and for breaches of data protection rules.[98]

Four states also took action. The Privacy Act 1975 in New South Wales established a Privacy Committee to 'make reports and recommendations to the Minister in relation to any matter that concerns the need for or the desirability of legislative or administrative action in the interests of the privacy of persons'. Western Australia and Victoria made references to their Law Reform Commission and Statute Law Revision Committee, while South Australia established a task force on the subject. As in other federal systems, particularly those of the United States and Canada, the constitutional division of powers would make it difficult for the federal government to legislate comprehensively to regulate in the interests of data protection in both the public and private sectors at the federal and state levels. Three of the six states have passed statutes to regulate surveillance.[99]

The federal Law Reform Commission reported in December 1983, recommending the creation of a federal Privacy Commissioner who would have the power to investigate complaints. This would be accompanied by a statutory right of access to personal information with procedures for correcting erroneous information. One particular development referred to in the report links data protection with transborder data flow issues. The report noted that offshore key punching in developing countries was used to save on costs, and that it made it more difficult for Australian law to protect the privacy of Australians.[100]

The federal Privacy Act was passed in 1988, strengthened from the bill introduced in 1986. That bill was introduced together with a proposal for a national identity card, the 'Australia card'. Opposition to the Australia card was such that it was withdrawn, and the Privacy Act provisions were made more strict. But the Act is still more like the US Privacy Act than a European data protection law. It only covers the public sector, and only at the federal (Commonwealth) level. The Act has 11 Privacy Principles, essentially the same as those in the OECD Guidelines or the Council of Europe Convention. Enforcement is by a combination of private action and action by the Privacy Commissioner, who can investigate and ask for injunctions against activity violating the Act, as well as receiving complaints. The Privacy Commissioner also has power to grant exemptions from the Act by making a Public Interest Declaration. There is no registration system, nor is there a requirement to give prior notice to data subjects. Instead there is a public register requirement that agencies make available for public inspection a record indicating the kind of personal data they process. There is one provision that affects the private sector by limiting the private sector use of the Tax File number.

The Privacy Protection Amendment Bill will extend the Commissioner's jurisdiction to the private sector to regulate credit reporting. The bill would establish principles of fair credit reporting and require the Commissioner to establish a legally enforceable Code of Conduct. Amendments to the Federal Crimes Act in 1989 extended the Commissioner's jurisdiction to deal with misuse of spent criminal conviction information. The Data Matching Program (Assistance and Tax) Act 1990 authorizes the establishment of data-matching programmes to detect fraud or tax evasion, but establishes interim guidelines for them.

The Freedom of Information Act 1982 establishes a general legal right of access to official federal government documents. Most importantly for the protection of privacy, it provides a right of access and of correction for personal files, whether automated or manual. The application to automatically processed information is specific under the provision of section 17 that if the agency 'could produce a written document by (i) the use of a computer that is ordinarily available to the agency for retrieving or collating stored information' there is an obligation to produce such a document on request.

Although the general right of access applies to any 'person', a request must specify an address in Australia for correspondence, and the right of correction only applies for Australian citizens and permanent residents.[101] The Act does not apply to documents created before it came into effect, although documents which are not more than five years old may be disclosed if they relate to the personal affairs of the person seeking access and if their disclosure is 'reasonably necessary' to understand documents which must be disclosed.[102]

Apart from the exemptions from access for specified reasons, there are also several classes of documents that are excluded from the operation of the Act entirely, including those of the Secret Service.[103] The exemptions with particular relevance to privacy include the security of the state, international relations, federal–state relations, confidential communications from the states, law enforcement, examinations, and the interests of third parties.

Documents are exempt in the interests of state security and international relations if their disclosure could reasonably be expected to cause damage to the 'security or the defense' of the country or to the country's international relations, or if it would divulge confidential communications from foreign governments.[104] The exemptions for damage to federal–state relations are similar to those under the Canadian legislation.[105]

The law enforcement exemptions resemble those in the US Freedom of Information Act. Section 37 makes a document exempt if its disclosure would prejudice investigations of law-breaking or failure to comply with tax laws, prejudice law enforcement in a particular case, disclose the identity of a confidential informant, endanger the lives or physical safety of people in connection with law enforcement, prejudice a fair trial, disclose lawful investigation methods, or prejudice public safety methods. Section 40's exemption for documents if their disclosure would prejudice the effectiveness of examinations and audits seems to have no specific equivalent in other countries' access laws.

The third-party exemption is important in terms of privacy, not only as a limit on subject access but also to protect the privacy of others. Section 41 provides that a document is exempt if disclosure would 'involve the unreasonable disclosure of information relating to the personal affairs of any person (including a deceased person)'. This, and a similar provision in the New Zealand Official Information Act, may be the only specific provisions to recognize the privacy of the dead in access legislation. The law, in section 41(2), makes it clear that this exemption cannot be relied upon to refuse a request for access to documents which relate only to the person making the request. If such a request is for medical or psychiatric information, and if it is thought that such access might be prejudicial to the subject's health, then access will only be given to a physician chosen by the subject.[106] There is also a 'personal commercial' exemption for information 'concerning a person in respect of his business or professional affairs ... if the disclosure would affect the lawful business or the professional, commercial, or financial affairs of that person'. There are also exemptions for documents protected by other specific secrecy statutes, lawyer–client privilege, or if disclosure would involve a breach of confidence.[107]

Countries with National Data Protection Laws only

Federal Republic of Germany

The Federal Republic of Germany is, like the USA, a federal republic with a written constitution guaranteeing fundamental human rights, and also has a considerable literature on the theory of privacy and several specific privacy protection remedies (discussed in the 1972 study). Although a right to privacy is not mentioned as such, the constitution begins with the statement that 'The dignity of man is inviolable. To respect and protect it shall be the duty of all state authority' (Article 1(1)). This is followed by other rights such as the one 'to the free development of his personality' (Article 2(1)) and the 'inviolability of his person' (Article 2(2)). Article 10 provides that

'Secrecy of the mail and secrecy of posts and telecommunications shall be inviolable. Restrictions may be ordered only pursuant to a law.' Article 13 spells out the conditions under which searches may be made in some detail.

(1) The home shall be inviolable.
(2) Searches may be ordered only by a judge or, in the event of danger in delay, by other organs as provided by law and may be carried out only in the form prescribed by law.
(3) Otherwise, this inviolability may be encroached upon or restricted only to avert a common danger or a mortal danger to individuals, or, pursuant to a law, to prevent imminent danger to public security and order, especially to alleviate the housing shortage, to combat the danger of epidemics or to protect endangered juveniles.

Some rights, including the right to secrecy of post and telecommunications, are forfeit if they are 'abused', in the words of Article 18, 'in order to combat the free democratic basic order'.

Probably the most significant judicial decision on information privacy, especially as it is affected by technology, was the ruling on 15 December 1983 by the federal Constitutional Court that the census which was to have taken place that year was unconstitutional.[108] Similar in effect to the US Supreme Court decision in *Griswold* v. *Connecticut*, but with far wider immediate implications, the decision was based on a constitutional right to 'informational self-determination'. The decision not only caused a revision and postponement of the census, but also led to delays in introducing a machine-readable identity card system.

The decision had been preceded by an injunction in April 1983 by which the Constitutional Court stopped the national census only two weeks before it was to begin. The Court based its decision on the basic 'personality rights' in Articles 2(1) and 1(1). These were not thought to forbid censuses as such, but required both a predominant public interest to justify a census and appropriate procedural safeguards. The compilation of statistics was acceptable so long as they were kept secret until all information by which they could be linked with individuals was eliminated. Most of the provisions of the census relating to statistical data were upheld, but the provision of the Census Act concerning residence registry was declared void. The objection to this registry was that data processing would make it comparatively easy to re-link the anonymous statistical data on housing with the name-related residence registry. This was one example of the Court's approach that automatic data processing means that there is no longer such a thing as insignificant data. It also declared void provisions of the Act which would have permitted distinguishing between staff and patients in mental homes, transmitting identifiable personal data from both federal and state statistical offices to other administrative agencies, and identifying religious affiliations.

The Court did not completely disapprove of the Census Act. The obligation to state one's religion on the census form was held to be consistent with the constitutional guarantee of freedom of religion, the obligation to give information about the home did not violate the Article 13 guarantee of home privacy, and the requirement to supply information did not violate the right to freedom of expression. The provision in the Census Act which allowed census data to be used for updating local authorities' registers of inhabitants was declared void. The Act contained a general data protection clause in section 11(7), which said that identifiable data should be erased immediately after use for purely statistical purposes. The Court held that this was inadequate, and that more procedural safeguards were required, although the details of such safeguards were not given.

The Court had earlier upheld the constitutionality of a 'micro-census'[109] which had the appropriate safeguards. The essence of the decision is that the rights guaranteed in Articles 1 and 2 include a relatively specific right of 'informational self-determination' which requires at least some data protection measures. In the commentaries on the decision it has even been doubted whether the federal Data Protection Act of 1977 fully complies with this requirement.[110]

Two international aspects of the case deserve mention, if only for the absence of commentary by the Court on them. The first is that the census was being carried out in compliance with two EEC direc-tives,[111] although the directives did not say how the census was to be conducted or what questions were to be asked, merely that it was to cover 'certain demographic, professional and social characteristics of individuals, households and families'. The effect of the decisions was that Germany failed to meet the requirement of the second directive that the census be held between 1 March and 31 May 1983. The second international aspect is the absence of any reference at all by the Court to the right of privacy under Article 8 of the European Convention on Human Rights or to the provisions of the Data Pro-tection Convention, which had been opened for signature over two years earlier, although it had not yet come into effect. Only a few months earlier, in October 1982, the Commission on Human Rights had found that the British census did not infringe Article 8 (see p. 27 above).

Although the German census decision is similar in style to that of the US Court in *Griswold*, the substance is rather different. One com-ment on the German decision may illustrate how the approaches of the two countries have diverged. It was said that 'the essence of the judgment lies in the recognition that data protection has now become indispensable for the protection of privacy, an idea which first germinated in the United States in the late 1960s'.[112] But the US Supreme Court has not yet said that the constitutional right to privacy requires data protection legislation, and the Privacy Act is rather different from German data protection legislation generally, particularly in its lack of private sector regulation and its lack of emphasis on data processing.

Germany has largely concentrated on legislation dealing with computers and privacy, beginning with the first such statute anywhere, in Hessen in 1970. This was followed by the federal government and eventually all of the Länder. The decision of the federal Constitutional Court in 1983 delaying the census on privacy grounds has no real counterpart in the United States. But there is no German equivalent, at the state or national level, to US legislation on rights of access to government information, and there seems to be little or no pressure for such legislation.

There was not much public pressure for the first data protection law in Hessen, at least nothing equivalent to the Safari affair in France or concerns over census information in several other countries. The National Commission of Lawyers said in 1970 that they favoured legislation on computers and privacy, and there was some academic writing on the subject. In Hessen, the Data Protection Bill was introduced in company with another bill to authorize a state and local data processing network. It was not exactly the price for the data processing bill, but it was appropriate to accompany a bill to extend public sector data processing with a measure to safeguard privacy. Most importantly, the Act established the office of Data Protection Commissioner, whose function was to advise the government and act as an ombudsman for data subjects. The Act was amended in 1978 after passage of the federal statute.

The federal Data Protection Act which became law in 1977 was not the first bill of its kind. A bill to regulate automatic and manual records in the public and private sectors was introduced in 1971, then withdrawn when the government announced a bill of its own. The government bill was intended to accompany another measure, rather like the legislation in Hessen. The federal measure was to introduce a national personal identification number to increase data processing efficiency, particularly in handling information about foreign residents. The provisions on personal registraion and the use of a PIN were rejected, however, while the Data Protection Bill was adopted.

The details of the federal and state data protection statutes are complicated, and the literature is considerable. But the basic division of jurisdiction is relatively simple. The federal Data Protection Act covers data processing of personal information in the private and the public sectors, but it is largely limited to regulating the public sector at the federal level. Although the federal statute might have some application to the states as they carry out federal functions, section 7(2) of the federal Act gives precedence to state law in such circumstances. State data protection laws primarily regulate the public sector at state levels, but there is a tendency towards special measures to regulate particular activities in the private sector, such as credit reporting.

At the federal level the Act requires that automated files in the public sector must be registered with the Federal Data Protection Commissioner, and that information about them be published in the official bulletin. Regulation of the private sector is very different from systems in many other countries such as those in Scandinavia and the United Kingdom: there is no general obligation to register. The principle of notice to data subjects is applied by other means, such as notice to the subject. Some categories of data processors who provide information as a commercial service must register.[113] There is a general right of subject access in both the public and private sectors, with further rights of correction and deletion. These are, however, not absolute.

At the federal public sector level, nearly all police, intelligence, military, prosecuting, and tax authorities are exempt from the requirement that they publish descriptions of their systems for handling personal data. They must, however, register with the Data Protection Commissioner, except for three agencies: the Federal Office for the Protection of the Constitution, the Federal Intelligence Service, and the Military Counter-Intelligence Service.[114]

There is no right of subject access to the files of any of these agencies, although the Data Protection Commissioner has a right to inspect them.[115] Quite apart from the exemption of those agencies from subject access, there are other general exemptions from subject access. These apply if access would be prejudicial to the functioning of the agency, if it would be prejudicial to the public security of the federal or of a state government, and if any other law requires that the information be kept secret.[116] These exemptions may justify refusal of access in the private sector as well.

Although the right of subject access and associated rights of correction can be seen as privacy protection measures, they may also interfere with the privacy of others. The federal act reflects this by providing an exemption in the public sector if the nature of the information requires that it not be disclosed because of an overriding and justified interest of a third person.[117] The private sector has similar exemptions from subject access if the disclosure of personal information would harm the overriding legitimate interests of a third party. There seems to be no special procedure by which the interests of the data subject and those of the third party can be presented, and the decisions as to which should prevail is made in the first instance by the data user.

The enforcement of German data protection legislation is complex of administrative supervision at the federal and state level, responsibility of designated corporate data protection officers in the private sector, and criminal offences for which fines and imprisonment may be imposed. These offences include failure to notify data subjects, failure to appoint a corporate data protection officer, and failure to give sufficient, correct, and timely information.[118]

One illustration of enforcement by state data protection commissioners comes from Nordrhein–Westfalen, where the commissioners disapproved of the common practice of local mayors in checking population registers for old age pensioners' birthdays in order to offer congratulations.[119]

Luxembourg

The constitution of Luxembourg guarantees 'natural rights', including guarantees that 'The domicile is inviolable. No domiciliary visit may take place except in the cases provided for by law and in the form which it prescribes' (Article 15). Article 28 provides that 'The secrecy of correspondence is inviolable. A law shall determine who are the agents responsible for the violation of the secrecy of letters confided to the mails. A law shall regulate the guaranty for the secrecy of telegrams.'

Luxembourg is a party to the European Convention on Human Rights. Although the Convention became a part of domestic law when it was ratified in September 1953 (and not when legislative approval to it was given earlier), the courts have not always found the Convention to prevail over conflicting domestic law. In at least two cases the Superior Court of Justice has considered the right to privacy under the Convention and the laws of Luxembourg. In a decision of 5 May 1975 the Court found that a motorist's rights under the Convention were not violated by taking a blood sample against his wishes.[120] A decision of 2 April 1980 applied the Convention right to privacy even more specifically. It annulled the order for telephone-tapping made by an investigating magistrate on the ground that it violated Article 8.[121] In another case the Cour de Cassation referred to the Court of Human Rights decision in the *Klass* telephone-tapping case.[122]

Luxembourg adopted a data protection law in 1979 to, in the words of a commission that reported in February of that year, 'protect natural or legal persons against the abusive use of data which concern them during the different phases of undergoing processing'. Privacy was to include legal as well as natural persons. The law is rather like the French data protection act, passed at about the same time (although France deleted the original provision for legal persons). There was also an access to government information law passed in the same year, but it bears little resemblance to the equivalent French statute. As it only gives a right of access to documents for those with a legal interest in them rather than being a general public right, it should not be classed with the laws generally referred to as 'freedom of information' acts.

There was not much public concern over computers and privacy leading to the legislation. In 1977 press reports that Luxembourg might become a 'data haven' for those trying to avoid German data protection laws were denied. It seems most likely that this tiny country decided to follow its neighbours in legislating, realizing that, with the Convention and OECD Guidelines being drafted, the prospect of maintaining corporate business without legislation would be unlikely.

The data protection law also accompanied the introduction of personal identification numbers for both natural and legal persons. These numbers were the keys to national registers of natural and legal persons established at the same time. This was to be administered by the state informatics centre (CIE), which was established in 1974 to promote and co-ordinate data processing.

The law protects both legal and natural persons, regulates both the public and private sector and does not cover manual records. It is administered by a Consultative Commission, but enforcement is largely ministerial. The basic principles are: compulsory authorization to process personal data automatically, creation of a national register of such processing, rights of access and correction for data subjects, regulation of data collection, inspection of personal data processing, and obligations of data processors.

Those who process personal data must automatically be authorized by the Consultative Commission. Information must be provided about the purpose of the processing, and where the information may be communicated must be provided, and the Commission may impose special conditions such as security measures. The Commission has some independence, but its only power is to recommend. The actual enforcement is by ministerial order (from the Minister of Transport, Communications and Informatics), with the possibility of appealing to the Conseil d'Etat.

Public sector processing of personal data must be authorized by statute or Grand Ducal regulation (roughly equivalent to a British Order in Council or a US Executive Order). Bills or regulations giving such authorization are first submitted to the Consultative Commission. Only the state may process police records, although petitions for bankruptcy may be processed in the private sector. Personal medical data may be processed only by medical authorities, social security organizations, and the public health department. It is forbidden to process personal data about political, trade union, religious or philosophical beliefs, as well as information about the 'intimacy of private life'.[123] Trade unions may process their membership records automatically, and union membership may be processed, but not communicated to third parties, with permission of the data subject.

When collecting personal information for automatic processing, the data subjects must be told the purpose of the collection, whether replies are compulsory, the consequences of refusing to answer compulsory questions, their rights of access and correction, and who may have access to the information.[124] The right of subject access begins with such notification, but the data subject may also consult a national register of data users without charge, and then exercise the right of access. There is no direct right of subject access to medical information, but it can be exercised through a doctor designated by the data subject. Otherwise, exemptions are specified by Grand Ducal regulation.

The access to information law of 8 June 1979 is somewhat similar to the French law in requiring reasons for administrative decisions. Essentially, it provides a right of access to an administrative file whenever a decision is taken which affects an individual. The person even has a right of deletion (rather than correction), in demanding that documents in the file which are prejudicial and irrelevant be removed.[125] But access may be refused if it would endanger security or invade the privacy of third parties. In such cases, a summary of the file which does not endanger security of privacy must be communicated, and the person concerned has the right to make observations on it.

In its 1983 report the Consultative Commission commented in particular about the practice of selling names and addresses from the telephone directory. The purpose of a telephone directory, it was emphasized, was to connect names with telephone numbers, and it was wrong to use it for other purposes. Similarly disapproved of was the practice of selling names and addresses of automobile owners to a direct-marketing firm in Belgium.[126]

The first Consultative Commission finished its five-year term in 1984 with a report which was highly critical of the apparent disregard of data protection by state bodies. Only 13 out of 22 public sector data banks had adopted any regulations at all. During its term the Commission had concentrated on public sector activities because it was felt that they were the most sensitive. Among other recommendations, the Commission had approved of the use of personal identifying numbers by local authorities, but not their use by private employers for anything other than dealing with tax and social security officials. The Commission urged the government to appoint a new body to enforce the Data Protection Act.

United Kingdom

Now, as in 1972, the United Kingdom has no general legal right to privacy. Few of the proposals of the Younger Committee have become law. Neither the courts nor Parliament have been particularly active in finding or making laws to protect privacy, with one major exception: under pressure from international institutions Parliament has legislated in the fields of data protection and interception of communication.

In terms of a general right to privacy almost nothing has changed, at least in terms of domestic law. (It should not be forgotten that Scotland's separate, and largely civil, legal system has gone further towards a general right to privacy through the principle of *actio injuriarum*, which provides a remedy for injuries to honour.)[127] The most effective provision of a general right to privacy was anticipated in the 1972 study, which noted that the United Kingdom was a party to the European Convention on Human Rights and had accepted the right of individual petition. 'It is conceivable, therefore, that a complaint could be brought before the European Commission in a proper case to enforce a right of privacy' (p. 458). That has happened, and in the cases of *Golder, Silver*, and *Malone*, already referred to in the discussion of European case law, the Court has enforced the right of privacy under Article 8 not only directly against the United Kingdom, but for all parties to the Convention. Although incorporation of the European Convention into domestic law could finally provide a general right to privacy enforceable in British courts, it might also deprive the institutions of the European Convention of a prime source of test cases.

There was no prediction in the 1972 study that the United Kingdom would legislate on the specific topic of data protection. By 1979 there had been sufficient progress for one observer to write that 'Given the inevitable international delays and pressure on the British government's legislative timetable, a reasonable projection would be for a bill to be introduced and passed during the 1982–83 session.' He concluded that 'It would perhaps be appropriate for a British Data Protection Act to take effect in 1984.' Events went more or less as predicted, despite the fact that the predictions were made before the Conservative government took power decisively in 1979.

The chronology of events which culminated in the Data Protection Act 1984 has been set forth in detail in other publications, and this will therefore be no more than an outline. The various bills to protect aspects of privacy during the 1960s were described in the 1972 study.

One of these private members' bills, which had been drafted by Justice, was introduced by Brian Walden, MP. He withdrew it in exchange for an undertaking from the Labour Home Secretary to appoint a committee to inquire into the protection of privacy. The committee was hampered in its enquiries by terms of reference restricting it to invasions of privacy in the private sector. Requests to both Labour and Conservative ministers to permit examination of threats to privacy from government were refused.

The Committee, chaired by Kenneth Younger, reported in 1972. Although the Committee did not favour a general right to privacy, a number of specific proposals were made. One of these was a set of principles to be observed in the automatic processing of personal data. Those principles deserve repetition not only for their influence on British privacy law, but also for their resemblance to the principles in the Council of Europe Data Protection Convention.

1. Information should be regarded as held for a specific purpose and not be used, without appropriate authorizsation, for other purposes; and
2. Access to information should be confined to those authorized to have it for the purpose for which it was supplied.
3. The amount of information collected and held should be the minimum necessary for the achievement of the specified purpose.
4. In computerized systems handling information for statistical purposes, adequate provision should be made in their design and programs for separating identities from the rest of the data.
5. There should be arrangements whereby the subject could be told about the information held concerning him.
6. The level of security to be achieved by a system should be specified in advance by the user and should include precautions against the deliberate abuse or misuse of information.
7. A monitoring system should be provided to facilitate the detection of any violation of the security system.
8. In the design of information systems, periods should be specified beyond which the information should not be retained.
9. Data held should be accurate. There should be machinery for the correction of inaccuracy and the updating of information.
10. Care should be taken in coding value judgements.

The development of data protection legislation at the international level has already been considered (see p. 32), but it seems fairly clear that British representatives at Council of Europe and OECD discussions took an active part in drafting, just as they had done in the drafting of the Council of Europe Convention on Human Rights. In domestic terms, the next specific development in legal protection of privacy was in the Consumer Credit Act 1974. The Younger Committee had recommended (in para. 298) that 'an individual should have a legally enforceable right of access to the information held about him by a credit rating agency'. (A similar recommendation had been made by the Molony Committee on consumer protection in 1970.) Just such a right was included in the 1974 Act, which had been introduced by a Conservative government and then re-introduced by the new Labour government.[128] The right of access in the Consumer Credit Act is to a transcript reduced into plain English, and so would almost certainly include computer-stored information, and require a print-out of it.[129] Appeals over rights of access, correction, and other questions (such as whether the 200-word statement to be included is 'scandalous' or not) are initially to the Director General of Fair Trading. One of the first acts of the new Labour Home Secretary was to travel to the United States to enquire into the Freedom of Information Act, which had just been amended, and the Privacy Act of 1974. He returned more convinced of the need for privacy legislation than for an open government law.

In 1975 the Labour government published two White Papers on computers and privacy. One of them[130] proposed a non-statutory body to prepare the way for permanent data protection machinery. That Data Protection Committee was announced early in 1976. There was a delay when the first chairman of the committee, Sir Kenneth Younger, died suddenly. A new chairman, Sir Norman Lindop, was appointed. The Committee reported in 1978.

The terms of reference for the Committee were to advise on legislation to protect personal data automatically processed. This meant that two issues on which other countries have differed in legislating on data protection, whether to include legal persons and manual records, were already decided. The committee was also directed to consider data protection in both the public and the private sectors.

The period between the publication of the Committee's report and legislation in 1984 was marked by a series of government announcements of policy short of what the Committee had recommended, followed by criticism from Sir Norman Lindop and other Committee members; after a period of silence the government then announced a change of mind to something closer to what had been recommended. In the end, most of the recommendations in the Lindop Report became law.

The structure of the proposed statute was to include an independent Data Protection Authority with broad regulatory powers. The government moved from an initial proposal that the Home Office should carry out these functions, through a single Registrar to be located in the Home Office, to the final Act's establishment of an entirely independent Registrar answerable only to Parliament, with considerable powers, from whom users may appeal to a special Tribunal. The Committee's proposals for the registration of data users were largely accepted. The Committee recommended that any exemption for reasons of national security should be 'precisely limited'; the Act allows for the complete exemption of any data processing if it is certified to be in the interests of national security by a cabinet minister. The Committee envisaged a major role for codes of practice in data protection. They were to be approved by Parliament and have the force of law. But the government resisted any recognition of such codes until the final legislative stages, when an amendment was allowed for the Registrar to encourage the development of voluntary codes.

The rules relating to medical and social welfare files were, however, effectively deferred beyond the Act and left to ministerial rule-making. Lindop had proposed that patient access to medical information should be considered, but left to a code of practice. The Act establishes a general rule of subject access, but leaves the rules for access to these kinds of information for later formulation. One particular aspect of data protection for employees seems not to have been considered specifically by Lindop. The report recommended that there should be no contracting-out from the provisions of the law. When the government bill was being considered in Parliament several amendments were put forward to stop the possibility that employers might require all applicants, and perhaps even all employees, to exercise their rights of subject access to records of any criminal convictions and give the results to employers as a condition of employment. All the proposals were rejected. In his 1990 annual report to the House of Commons the Registrar said that there was 'growing evidence that employers are asking prospective employees to provide them with a copy of their criminal record, which they can obtain from the police'. The Home Affairs Committee agreed with him that this was 'a misuse of the Data Protection Act.'[131]

The Data Protection Act 1984 would almost certainly not have been enacted had it not been for apprehensions that the United Kingdom needed legislation in order to ratify the Council of Europe Convention, and that other national data protection laws might be used as non-tariff trade barriers if the United Kingdom did not ratify. The bill was presented as having the two objectives of protecting privacy and promoting trade in data processing, but the responsible minister conceded, in a speech to a Canadian audience, that he was only persuaded of the need for legislation by the economic argument.[132] In the event, the Act was passed in a form which precluded the United Kingdom from ratifying the Convention for two years after the Act went into effect, since the Registrar's principal powers, and the right of subject access, were suspended during that period to allow time for mass registration to take place. Article 4 of the Convention requires each Party to take the necessary measures for data protection 'at the latest at the time of entry into force of this Convention in respect of that Party'. In fact, the Convention entered into force in the autumn of 1985, three months after deposit of the fifth instrument of ratification, so the United Kingdom remained outside the data protection 'club' for the first two years.

It was thus international law in the form of the Data Protection Convention, which derives in part from the right to privacy under Article 8 of the European Convention on Human Rights, that caused the United Kingdom to adopt its data protection legislation. Similarly, it was a decision of the European Court of Human Rights that persuaded the United Kingdom to adopt legislation to regulate the interception of communication. In the *Malone* case, already discussed under the law of the European Convention, the Court held unanimously that both the system of telephone interception and of providing 'metering' information to the police violated the right to privacy.

The application was brought by a man named Malone who had been tried and acquitted on charges of handling stolen property. During his trial he discovered that his telephone had been tapped. This in itself was unusual, as direct evidence of intercepted conversations is never used in court as a matter of administrative practice. After his acquittal he brought a civil action against the Metropolitan Police Commissioner. The action failed because there is no general right to privacy and because none of his particular claims provided a remedy. In particular, the law of confidence, the articulation of which in *Prince Albert* v. *Strange* is nearly as familiar in privacy literature as the Warren and Brandeis article, was held not to apply to intercepted communications. The Vice-Chancellor did consider Article 8 of the European Convention and its interpretation in the *Klass* case, but could not apply it because the Convention had not yet been incorporated into British law. He did, however, say that the subject was one which 'cried out' for legislation.[133]

Having exhausted his domestic remedies, Malone exercised his right of individual petition to the European Commission of Human Rights. In addition to his claim that tapping his telephone, which the police had conceded having done at least once, violated his Article 8 right, Malone also claimed that his right to privacy had been violated by police use of 'metering' information. He claimed that police had used information from this source about the people he had telephoned, and that several people he had talked to had been visited by the police. The government denied that any metering had taken place, and argued further that no privacy issue was presented if it had, because the information would only be a record of signals sent to the exchange, and not from any conversation.

The Commission found in Malone's favour on the question of whether the British system of telephone-tapping had violated his right to privacy, but they could not find any violation of his rights by metering because there was inadequate evidence from which they could find that his telephone had been metered or that such information was ever furnished to the police. The case was then referred to the Court, which had before it not only the arguments of Malone and the British government, but also written observations from the Post Office Engineering Union, which had been given permission under the Court's new rules. The POEU submission included evidence that metering information was given to the police without any judicial or administrative warrant.

In August 1984 the Court's judgment was published. The Court held unanimously that there had been a breach of Article 8 both regarding the interception of communication and the release of metering records to the police. In keeping with its usual approach the Court first considered whether there had been an interference with the right to privacy, then considered whether it had been authorized by law. They found that it had not been so authorized, and so did not enquire further into whether the interference was justified in a democratic society for one of the reasons listed in paragraph 2 of Article 8. They also felt it unnecessary to consider whether there had been a violation of Article 13, which guarantees a right to an effective domestic remedy for violations of rights guaranteed by the Convention. Two partially dissenting opinions and one concurring opinion urged that the Court go further and indicate what the Convention required as an effective domestic remedy for invasions of privacy.

The British government acted quickly, introducing a bill to regulate the interception of communication. That bill became the Interception of Communication Act 1985. In outline, the law gives legislative approval to the existing system of ministerial warrants. However, a quasi-judicial system of review was introduced in the form of a tribunal. Anyone who suspects an interference with communication may appeal to the tribunal, which has wide powers to investigate. If they find that there has been an interception which was not properly authorized, they have the power to order that it be stopped, that records be destroyed, and that damages be paid. But if they find that the interception was properly authorized they will report to the applicant only that they have found no violation. Although it is not absolutely clear from the statute whether the tribunal may inquire into whether the ministerial warrant was actually justified under the Act, the minister said that they could.

In at least one sense the Act extends the scope of permissible intercepts. The existing administrative system was said to have been used only for the prevention and detection of serious crime, with definitions of serious crime varying somewhat over the years. The Act incorporates this standard for domestic intercepts. However, the

Act also authorizes what may be called 'class' intercepts for international communications. One ground for such intercepts, which are
wider in scope than domestic ones, is the prevention of terrorism.
Another allows international interceptions in the interests of the 'economic well-being of the country'. This does not necessarily require
any evidence of violation of the criminal law. The words are, of
course, taken directly from the second paragraph of Article 8. Although it is likely that the words were adopted originally in the
interests of countries with exchange controls being able to intercept
communications for evidence of violations of those controls, the phrase
does not necessarily require such violations. The United Kingdom
does not now have exchange controls, and it is at least possible,
under the new law, for the British government to inform its economic
strategy by the interception of international financial communications. The Act also contains an absolute ban on the introduction of
any evidence in any judicial proceeding other than before the tribunal to indicate that an interception has taken place.

The law of confidence, important in the historical development of
privacy, thought by the Younger Committee to be an important potential doctrine for the protection of privacy, but insufficient to provide Mr Malone with a remedy, may be given new statutory form.
One of the few recommendations of the Younger Committee to be
acted upon was the proposal that the Law Commissions (one for
England and Wales, the other for Scotland) should consider the doctrine and its possible reform. The Lord Chancellor referred the matter to both Commissions, who considered it over the years. While the
law was being considered by them it was being used in novel ways,
particularly in efforts by the government to prevent unauthorized
disclosures of government information. The Law Commission for
England and Wales reported in 1981.[134]

The Law Commission proposals are a mixture of greater protection for individual privacy and measures to allow greater freedom of
the press under the doctrine, which would be made a statutory tort.
The greater protection for privacy would be in the extension of the
obligation of confidentiality to information obtained by surveillance.
This was in part to reverse the statement by Megarry V.-C. in *Malone*
that a person who uses a telephone must accept the risk of being
overheard by tapping. The Commission commented that they did
'not think that in a civilized society a law-abiding citizen using the
telephone should have to expect that it may be tapped'.[135]

The Commission's draft bill would impose such an obligation for
information obtained without authority from any computer or data
retrieval system. It would also impose the obligation for information
obtained by a device made primarily for the purpose of surreptit-
iously carrying out surveillance, or for any other device capable of

being used for such purpose. The 'ordinary' surveillance device, such as a camera with a telephoto lens, is made subject to a 'reasonable expectation' test: acquisition of information by such a device imposes an obligation of confidentiality only if 'a reasonable man in the position of the person from whom the information is acquired would have appreciated the risk'.

> Thus, on the one hand, it may be thought that two people, who meet secretly in a secluded corner of a large railway station throughout which clear notices are displayed that television cameras are being used to deter criminal activities (such as malicious damage), cannot reasonably expect the fact of their meeting to be treated as confidential. On the other hand, it may well be that the use of an ordinary camera with a telephoto lens to obtain from the street a picture of a confidential document lying on a desk in a private house would go far beyond the reasonable expectations of the person who left it there, and that the taker of the picture should be subject to an obligation of confidence in respect of the information so obtained.[136]

The provision for the freedom to receive and impart information lay in the changes made to the existing doctrine that breaches of confidentiality may be justified in the public interest. In its present form this is a defence to an action for breach of confidence on the basis that the breach was justified to disclose 'iniquity', which until recently was largely restricted to justifying disclosure of crime. The Commission expanded this, recommending that the 'public interest may arise in the disclosure or use of confidential information whether or not the information relates to iniquity or other forms of misconduct'.[137] The other important change is that if the person accused of a breach of confidence satisfies the court that the public interest is involved, then 'it should be for the plaintiff to establish that this interest is outweighed by the public interest in the protection of the confidentiality of the information'.[138]

The government has undertaken to introduce legislation based on the Law Commission report, although it may not necessarily take the form of the Commission's draft bill. It will go some way towards increasing the legal protection for some privacy interests, but it is not, as the Commission pointed out, a protection of privacy measure: 'to give a remedy merely because information is acquired by one of these means [by surveillance device] would amount to the creation of a right of privacy – a right, for example, not to be photographed even if the photographs were later never published'.[139]

To create such a right was almost certainly beyond the Commission's terms of reference, but their proposals and analysis raise fundamental questions about the legal protection of privacy. Is it the initial obtaining of information (which one person prefers to keep private) by another person an invasion of privacy? The answer may be an easy 'yes' if it is assumed that the person observed becomes aware of it. It is more difficult if the obtaining of information is by the surreptitious methods contemplated by the Commission, which are designed not to reveal the fact of observation to the person observed. Imposing an obligation of confidentiality on information so obtained is important, but it limits the public use of that information rather than the activity of surveillance itself. That may depend on the interpretation given to the principle in Article 5 of the Data Protection Convention, which says that 'personal data undergoing automatic processing shall be obtained and processed fairly and lawfully'.

Although all opposition parties have now endorsed a Freedom of Information Act, the Conservative government is so firmly opposed that it resorted to unprecedented pressure to vote down such a bill introduced by a Conservative member of the House of Commons in 1988. The Freedom of Information Campaign has been successful with several sectoral bills, some of which are specifically privacy protection measures. The Access to Personal Information Act gives rights of subject access to various social services records, and the Access to Medical Records Act gave patients rights of access to their medical records from November 1991.

Ireland

The Irish Data Protection Act 1988 covers automated records, public and private sectors, and emphasizes self-regulation by requiring registration only by specified organizations holding sensitive data. These include the entire public sector, financial institutions, agencies dealing with credit information, debt collecting, direct marketing, and computer bureaux. The Act is similar to the British Act, but uses 'data controller' instead of 'data user' to describe the person who controls the content and use of personal data. The Data Protection Commissioner is required to encourage the preparation of codes of conduct, which may be given the force of law by Parliament. The principles are those of the Council of Europe Convention, and the main exemption from the right of subject access is if it would prevent the investigation of criminal offences. The Act came into force in 1989.

Austria

The Austrian constitution includes a procedure by which statutes may be given the status of 'constitutional' laws. This was done with the laws of 1862 and 1867 which guaranteed rights to the inviolability of the home and secrecy of correspondence. Not only does the Convention have effect in domestic law by virtue of the Austrian doctrine of automatic incorporation, it has also been given the status of a constitutional law.[140] In at least one case the Constitutional Court has held that interference with private life is not justified by immorality unless the interference also is 'necessary in a democratic society'.

The right to privacy guaranteed by Article 8 of the European Convention is generally applicable in Austrian domestic law because the Convention is incorporated into Austrian law. The Austrian data protection legislation was intended to give particular effect to this general right in connection with personal data, and the Act creates a basic right to data protection under Austrian constitutional law: 'Any person shall have the right to demand that personal data concerning him be kept secret, provided that he has an interest warranting protection therein, notably as concerns respect for his private and family life'. [141]

The Act did not become law until 1978, but it was first announced in 1971. Although the announcement was in the same year as the census, there seems not to have been anything like the degree of concern about computers and privacy that prompted similar legislation in other countries. Rather, it seems to have been the product of concern over compliance with the Convention on Human Rights and the example of the Federal Republic of Germany, a neighbouring federal state, legislating on the subject at about the same time.

The Austrian legislation is different in several important ways from the German equivalent. It is a federal statute which effectively occupies the field of data protection, although there remains some room for possible legislation by the states. It covers both public and private sector data processing, gives rights to both natural and legal persons, and has some application to manual as well as automated records. The Austrian enforcement procedure is a combination of an administrative commission, administrative courts, the ordinary courts, and a Data Protection Council to oversee the implementation of the Act. The decision to include legal with natural persons in the Act was a conscious one, with the reasoning explained in an explanatory note: 'most data on a legal person may be reduced to information on natural persons; and on the other hand data processing poses a threat also to collective interests'. It seems, however, that the extension of rights to legal persons is not as complete as in Denmark, Norway, and Luxembourg, with its application limited to those legal persons which are businesses subject to the Commercial Code.[142]

The basic structure of administrative regulation by the Commission is tied to the responsible person, that is, the person responsible for the data processing, which can be translated as 'automation-supported data transactions' (*automationsunterstürtztes Datenverkehr*). This may be an expansive definition, including all phases of processing data if a single phase of processing is automatic. The system of regulation is similar for public and private sectors, with some differences.

Regulation in the public sector is by the Data Protection Commission, with judicial review in the administrative courts. Collection and processing of personal data in the public sector must be based on an explicit statutory authorization or an implied authorization if such processing is an 'essential prerequisite' to a statutory function. The basic rights of subject access and correction do not apply to data processing for purposes of national defence and law enforcement. The scope of these exemptions, as well as the measures to be taken in place of subject access, is determined by the Data Protection Commission. Disclosure of personal data must be justified by explicit statutory authority, written consent of the data subject, disclosure of financial obligations for credit purposes, disclosure for statistical purposes in anonymous form, implicit statutory authority for performance of a statutory duty, or after 'appropriate measures' if the data subject cannot be located.

Regulation of data processing in the private sector requires some legitimate objective for the processing of personal data, which must be balanced against the interest of the data subject which deserves protection. There is a distinction between most processing of personal data and what may be called 'internal' processing of personal data concerning those with whom the processor has a contractual relationship. This would seem to be largely, although not entirely, data about employees. Disclosure of such data is permitted only if it is required by law, in the course of payment, or with the express consent of the data subject for disclosure to identified parties. Also, direct notice of processing to the data subject may be substituted for notice via the public register. Disclosure of other personal data processed in the private sector is governed by different standards, including disclosure necessary to protect 'overriding and legitimate interests of third parties'.

The basic right of the data subject is the constitutional right previously mentioned to have personal data kept secret. This is subject to disclosures to protect third parties and a general provision allowing disclosures when provided for by law if they are required 'in the interests of national security, public safety, the economic well-being of the country, the prevention of disorder or crime, the protection of health and morals, or the protection of the rights and freedoms of others'. These reasons are taken directly from the Convention's list of justifiable interferences with the Article 8 right to privacy. The additional provision for disclosures in the interests of third parties seems to repeat the Convention's justification to protect the rights and freedoms of others.

The data subject's rights regarding automatically processed personal data begin with the right to know of the processing. This may be through the public register of such processing in both the public and private sectors. For some kinds of 'internal' processing, direct notice to the data subject may be substituted. In addition, the data subject has the right, on request, to be told who is in charge of the data processing, where the data are obtained from, what is processed, and what it is used for. Once the right of subject access is exercised, the data subject has the right to know to whom the data have been communicated. In addition to the right of correction for clearly inaccurate data, there is also a right to have a note that the data subject disputes the accuracy of other data. The major difference between the public and private sectors is that subject access in the public sector may be refused on the basis of an 'overriding public interest' under law, while refusal in the private sector can be based on an 'overriding legitimate interest of the person responsible or a third party'. Although the Data Protection Commission advises the government on exemptions from the right to notice and the rights of subject access and correction, it is not clear whether the Commission then acts on behalf of a data subject in reviewing such exempt information. The Commission does have a general power of investigation and recommendation in the public sector, and a department must give reasons for not accepting a recommendation. In addition to the citizen's right of access and correction, there is an additional civil remedy of compensation for damages through the ordinary civil court.[143]

The Data Protection Commission has four members appointed for five-year terms. The Commission is a combination of regulatory body and administrative court. Its regulatory functions are largely with the private sector, where it can deny registration applications. In the public sector one of the Commission's main functions is to consider complaints that rights have been violated, with further possible appeals to the regular administrative courts. The Council is an unusual body in comparative data protection law. Its 15 members represent nearly all political bodies and levels of government. Its function is entirely advisory, but includes the drafting of proposed amendments to the basic law.

Quite apart from data protection, Austria adopted a 'Credit Act' in 1979 which provides criminal penalties to protect banking secrecy. There are limited exceptions to this rule for the disclosure of information in the course of criminal trials, criminal tax proceedings, and to a trustee in bankruptcy. Other disclosures of banking information require the explicit written consent of the client.

Austria does not have anything approaching the kind of public access to information legislation in countries such as France, but in 1973 it did enact a duty on federal ministers to inform the public and to ensure that their subordinates did the same. This does not apply to the states, even when they are engaged in implementing federal functions, and it is subject to the more basic constitutional principle of administrative secrecy. In the guidelines which implement the duty to inform it is made clear that there is no right of access to documents; as in equivalent legislation in the Netherlands, there is only a duty to communicate the contents of official documents. There is a clear right of appeal to the administrative courts, however.

Iceland

Iceland's constitution is similar to that of Denmark, with which it was joined in varying degrees of union for over a thousand years. Article 66 provides that: 'The home shall be inviolate. Houses may not be searched, nor any letters or other documents be detained and examined, except by judicial warrant or by a special provision of law.' Iceland is a party to the European Convention on Human Rights, but the Convention has not been incorporated into domestic law. Nor does it seem to have acquired much persuasive effect in the courts. In what seems to be the only case testing a claim to privacy under the Convention in Iceland, a man appealed to the Supreme Court arguing that regulations prohibiting the keeping of dogs in one's home in Reykjavik violated his right to privacy. On 18 June 1975 the Court rejected his claim, saying that the Convention had not been given the force of domestic law and, in any case, the prohibition on dogs was not a violation of Article 8. When he later applied to the European Commission of Human Rights in 1976 the Commission agreed, and found his application inadmissible.[144]

The Icelandic Data Protection Act of 1981 which came into effect in 1982 is almost an exact copy of the Danish Act, particularly in the protection given to legal persons. It expired at the end of 1985, and was replaced by a revised law which came into force in January 1986. That in turn was replaced by an Act Concerning the Registration and Handling of Personal Data that came into force at the beginning of 1990. The law has special provisions for opinion polls and market research. This requires that information obtained by an opinion poll must be deleted immediately or stored in such a way as to make identification of individuals impossible. Otherwise it makes no basic changes.

The law regulates both the public and private sectors. Licences are required for activities such as processing information on financial status or credit rating for communication to third parties, to operate computer service bureaux, or to process information for use abroad. Statutory authority and proof of necessity is required to process information on race, colour, political or religious convictions, criminal records, sexual conduct, health records, and use of alcohol. Licences for processing health and related information are only granted to medical doctors and hospitals.

The law is enforced by an independent three-member Data Committee, which grants licences and decides disputes. Decisions of the Committee cannot be appealed. Two appeals are particularly relevant to personal information privacy. Just as 35 per cent of people in the United Kingdom objected to having their names and addresses on the electoral register,[145] two Icelandic voters objected to having their names on the equivalent register in that country. One objection apparently was directed at the use of such registers by poll-watchers from political parties, while the other simply wanted his name removed. Both failed because of the statutory authority for such a register.[146]

Israel

Israel's privacy act of 1981 is a general privacy protection measure and data protection law in a single package. The first part of the law lists in some detail the kind of behaviour which can amount to an invasion of the right to privacy when it is carried out by those outside government. These include intercepting telephone conversations, surreptitious recording, filming or photography, and publishing information obtained in confidence. These are criminal offences, with sentences of one year's imprisonment, with an additional possibility of civil remedies.

The second part of the law is a data protection measure. The pattern of regulation is a familiar one, with a registrar who can refuse registrations, subject to judicial appeals. The enforcement is almost entirely judicial, including the right of subject access and the right to correction of erroneous information.

This is not the first Israeli law relating to privacy, but it is the first attempt at a comprehensive statute. A law was passed in 1974 creating a tort of using a person's image or name without permission for commercial purposes.[147] This, like equivalent laws in other countries and in some US states, only regulated the use of such images, not the act of surreptitious photography. The Kahn Committee was appointed in 1974 to consider the protection of privacy, and it reported in 1976, recommending a single statute to establish a broad right to privacy.[148] The first bill to be introduced was a measure to restrict aural surveillance. The Secret Monitoring Act of 1979 makes it a criminal offence to listen to the conversation of another by means of an instrument, including recording such a conversation. Such 'monitoring' is a criminal offence unless it is done with a permit issued for the purposes of state security or to detect or prevent crime.[149]

The government bill based on the Kahn Committee Report was introduced in 1980 and became law the next year. It does not attempt a general definition of privacy, but lists circumstances which would constitute an infringement (in contrast to the Kahn Committee approach, which was to establish a general right with the circumstances merely as examples upon which the courts could expand). The circumstances are similar to those of the Nordic declaration and the UN recommended points. They include: listening-in prohibited under any law (such as the 1979 Act), photographing a person while he is in the private domain, spying on a person in a manner likely to harass him, breaching a legal duty of secrecy relating to a person's private affairs, and copying a letter not intended for publication without permission. It is also an infringement to publish a person's photograph if it is likely to humiliate him (apparently in addition to the existing law on commercial use), or to publish anything about a person's 'intimate life, state of health or conduct in the private domain'. These last two are subject to the defence that the publication was justified in the public interest and that it was not 'mendacious'.[150] There is another defence if the infringement is committed in good faith where there is a legal, moral, social, or professional obligation to do so.[151] This is subject to a particular provision rather like the English Law Commission's proposed shift in the burden of proof as to the public interest in their proposed law of confidence. If the infringement is established to have been in fulfilment of such a duty and not excessive, the burden of proving bad faith shifts to the other party.[152]

The other party in such a case may be a plaintiff or a prosecutor, as the law makes infringements not only civil wrongs but also criminal offences. The civil remedy is compensation and possible confiscation of any infringing matter.[153] The criminal offence requires wilfulness, and the maximum sentence is one year's imprisonment.[154] The criminal prosecution may be brought by the aggrieved individual, although the state retains the right to take over the prosecution.[155]

The data protection section requires registration for anyone responsible for a database which processes information regarding the personality, personal status, intimate affairs, state of health, economic position, vocational qualifications, or opinions and beliefs of an individual.[156] A registrar is appointed, and is subject to appeals to the courts. He must accept registrations unless he has reasonable cause to believe that the database is to be used for illegal activities. It is an offence to use such information for any purpose except that for which the database was established or the information was intended, with a year's imprisonment as the maximum penalty.

The law also provides a right of subject access. This is subject to an exemption for medical records if there are said to be medical reasons for withholding it. There is a right to have information amended or deleted if it is incorrect or out of date, with a right of appeal to the courts. Requests for subject access may be refused for reasons of security or foreign relations.

Section 19 provides a relatively wide security and law enforcement exemption. There is no liability for any act done under authority of law, and no liability for any infringement committed by a security authority or any person acting on its behalf. 'Security authority' includes the police, the military, and the security services.[157]

The Israeli approach is roughly as if the British Parliament had accepted the idea of a general right to privacy, then limited it largely to the specific circumstances for which the Younger Committee proposed remedies, and incorporated the recommendations of the Lindop Committee as well. Apart from the provisions for subject access, the law does not follow the pattern of French and Canadian legislation in establishing general rights of access to information, but it is otherwise an omnibus law (with, it must be said, something approaching an omnibus law enforcement and security exemption).

Portugal

Portugal is, with Spain, notable for including in its constitution specific provisions not just for the protection of privacy, but for the protection of privacy in the context of computerized handling of personal data. Article 33 of the 1975 Constitution established the general right to privacy as the 'right to identity, a good name, and privacy':

> 1. Everyone shall have the right to his personal identity, to his good name and reputation and to privacy in his personal and family life.
> 2. Effective safeguards against the wrongful use, or use contrary to human dignity, of information concerning persons and families shall be provided by law.

Article 34 concerns the 'inviolability of home and correspondence':

> 1. The individual's home and the privacy of his correspondence and other means of private communication shall be inviolable.
> 2. A citizen's home shall not be entered against his will except by order of the competent judicial authority and in the cases and according to the forms laid down by law.
> 3. No one shall enter the home of any person at night without his consent.

4.   Any interference by public authority with correspondence or tele-communications, apart from the cases laid down by law in connection with criminal procedure, shall be prohibited.

Article 35 concerns 'use of data processing':

1.   All citizens shall have the right to information on the contents of data banks concerning them and on the use for which it is intended. They shall be entitled to require the said contents to be corrected and brought up to date.
2.   Data processing shall not be used for information concerning a persons's political convictions, religious beliefs or private life except in the case of non-identifiable data for statistical purposes.
3.   Citizens shall not be given all-purpose national identification numbers.

One writer commented that these provisions 'suffer the vice of vague-ness because the constitution does not define the term 'privacy'.[158]

In February 1989 the Constitutional Court ruled that legislation was required to implement this provision, and the amended consti-tution in that year revised Article 35 as follows:

1.   With the exception of the law on State secrecy and Justice secrecy, all citizens shall have the right to information contained in automated data records or files concerning themselves and to the use which it is intended. They shall be entitled to request that the contents be cor-rected and brought up to date.
2.   The access to personal data records or files shall be forbidden for purposes of getting information about third parties as well as the interconnection of these files save in exceptional cases as provided for in the law ...
3.   Data processing shall not be used for information concerning a person's philosophical or political convictions, party or trade union affiliations, religious beliefs or private life except in the case of non-identifiable data for statistical purposes.
4.   The law defines the concept of personal data for purposes of data storage as well as the conditions of establishing data banks and databases by public or private entities and the conditions of utiliz-ation and access.
5.   Citizens shall not be given all-purpose national identification num-bers.
6.   The law defines the provisions applicable to the transborder data flows establishing adequate norms or protection of personal data and of any other data in which the national interest is justified.

Although it is contained under the article on 'freedom of expression and information' (37), the constitution also provides that: '4.   The right of reply shall be equally and effectively secured to all natural and artificial persons.'

Several bills to establish data protection authorities have been prepared, and the Protection of Personal Data Act finally became law in 1991. In 1984 it was announced that Portugal intended to ratify the Council of Europe Convention, and that a committee to reconcile the differences between two draft bills had been appointed. An earlier bill had been drafted by the Social Democrats in 1978, and there was even a draft clause in the constitution which would have required legislation to establish a data protection commission.

The bill that was finally adopted covers automated records concerning natural persons in the public and private sectors. It establishes a National Commission for the Protection of Automated Personal Data, which enforces rights of subject access and correction. The Commission has sweeping powers to ban interconnection of automated files, to ban the use of a personal identification number to interconnect files with 'sensitive' data, and to require the destruction of data that is no longer required. The Act, unlike the law in the Netherlands, creates many criminal offences, not all of them connected with information technology. Creating an unauthorized file is an offence, as is the offence of unauthorized destruction of personal data or attempting to gain entry to a personal data information system. It is also an offence to reveal 'personal data ... putting in jeopardy the reputation, honour and esteem or the intimacy of another individual's private affairs'.[159]

Japan

Japan passed a national Personal Data Protection Act in 1988, and many of the prefectures and municipalities have ordinances on the subject. Article 13 of the 1946 Constitution says that 'All the people shall be respected as individuals,' which has been interpreted as a constitutional right to privacy. The most celebrated civil case on the right to privacy was brought by a politician who, in 1964, successfully sued the novelist Yukio Mishima for writing a thinly-disguised novel about him.

In the field of data protection, legislation followed the report of a government committee, the Study Committee on the Protection of Privacy, chaired by Professor Kato of Tokyo University. The Kato Report in 1982 proposed a law based on the OECD principles, but it was first acted upon at the local level. After other committee reports, a bill was introduced in 1988 and became law in 1989. The Act only applies to national public sector administrative bodies, although efforts have been made to adopt voluntary codes of conduct in the private sector. The right of subject access and correction is established, but is subject to several exceptions for matters concerning school examinations and records, medical treatment and law enforcement.[160]

Although Japan does not have a national access to information act, many prefectures and municipalities have adopted such ordinances. The best known, and the model for many others, is the Kanagawa Prefecture Disclosure of Information Ordinance. Although reports of the decisions of its Review Board on Official Documents Disclosure seem very much like most cases from other countries on access to government information such as minutes of meetings, there seems to be little use of such local legislation for subject access.

Countries with Access to Government Information Laws only

Greece

Greece passed an access to administration documents law in 1986,[161] and amended it in 1991. It is very similar to the French statute, establishing a general right to inspect and copy government records unless they concern the private or family life of third persons. The grounds for exemption from such access seem broader than those in the French law, however. The usual exemptions in such legislation are included: for national defence, foreign policy, detection of crime, commercial confidentiality, and secrecy obligation otherwise established by law. Somewhat broader exemptions are provided for documents concerning the internal debates of ministers and other governmental bodies and public confidence in the currency. Other exemptions may be proclaimed by the President and the responsible minister. The law is silent on the crucial question of what independent arbiter can decide whether a particular document is exempt, and there seem to be no decided cases.

The subject access provision is at least explicit, by providing that personal privacy, medical secrecy, or commercial secrecy cannot be used to refuse access to a citizen who is the subject of the document. However, like many but not all access laws, medical information cannot be communicated directly, but only through an appointed doctor.

The law is apparently not widely used. It is like the French law in prohibiting the reuse of information obtained by exercising the right of access for commercial purposes, and this has been interpreted as grounds for refusing to disclose information if it is to be used commercially.[162]

A government data protection bill was published in 1987, but seems unlikely to be adopted in the near future. But there is a privacy protection measure in connection with identity cards under the law on the relationship between the citizen and the state.[163] The law prohibits the linking of information in various databases, such as the population register, electoral register, tax register, social insurance and register of driving licences, and provisionally applies the principles of data protection until legislation is enacted. The use of the personal identification number (EKAM) for such purposes is specifically prohibited.[164]

Countries with Constitutional Privacy Provisions only

Spain

Spain, like Portugal, has a specific reference to data processing in its constitution. Part 4 of Article 18 says: 'Law will limit the use of data processing in order to safeguard personal honour, integrity, and relationships of citizens.' Part 3 says that 'Postal, telegraph, and telephone communication secrecy is established, unless a judicial order exists to the contrary.'

Spain ratified the Council of Europe Convention in 1984, in anticipation of the passage of a data protection bill the same year. But political difficulties have meant that it was not until July 1991 that a bill was introduced in the parliament (the Cortes), and was adopted in 1992. The bill follows the usual European pattern of establishing principles applicable to data processing in the public and private sectors and creating a Data Protection Agency to enforce them. The Agency is to be assisted by a Consultative Board of representatives from public and private sector groups. It provides for subject access and rights of correction for natural persons. In a slightly unusual provision it authorizes the government to extend protection to legal persons and societies after a report from the Data Protection Agency. It does not apply to manual records.

Other Countries

The spread of data protection legislation since 1972 has been one of the more interesting phenomena in comparative law. In that year there were no national or local laws that could be described as 'data protection' laws. There were national and local laws establishing general public rights of access to administrative documents, and the subject access that those provided could be described as a form of data protection. But in 1972 such laws only existed in Sweden, the United States, Finland (in rather weak form) and Norway and Denmark (both of which had only just legislated). The first national data protection law was in Sweden in 1973, with the *Land* of Hesse legislating the same year. Now there are at least 18 countries with national data protection laws (although some, like the USA and Canada, apply only to the public sector), and many more are in the process of legislating.

In European data protection circles it has been suggested that a government intent on resisting the trend toward data protection legislation should host a Council of Europe colloquy on the subject. Three have been held thus far, at Rome in 1982, Madrid in 1985, and Athens in 1987. At each colloquy the host government presented its data protection proposals.

Belgium and Switzerland also seem likely to legislate very soon. Belgium has been considering legislation for several years, and the bill introduced in May 1991 was adopted in 1992 and took effect in various stages in 1993. Switzerland has a Federal Data Protection Office that prepared the bill now before the national parliament, and already advises on the application of data protection principles to measures such as health information cards. Concern in Switzerland was heightened in the late 1980s by the 'Files Affair', in which a federal commission investigating the case of a minister who was charged with breach of official secrecy law (and acquitted) revealed the extent of surveillance of the population recorded in the dossiers of the security service.

Another country that is in the process of introducing a data protection bill, and where the constitutional court has been interpreting the right to privacy and its violation by the use of personal identification numbers would not have been predicted even five years ago: Hungary.

European 'Socialist' Countries

One of the characteristics of totalitarian countries of the left or right is the surveillance of populations. The pace of dramatic events in Eastern Europe makes it difficult to present an accurate description of the law and practice regarding privacy and informatics in those countries. It is, however, worth attempting to illustrate how countries in which legal rights to privacy which formerly had no real meaning are coping with the dismantling of state surveillance systems.

The existence of files maintained by the security services poses difficult questions for such countries. Most of them, it appears, are manual systems, which perhaps demonstrates that information technology does not create the problem, but changes its scale. In what was the German Democratic Republic, in what was the Czech and Slovak Federation, and in Bulgaria, serious questions have been raised about the future use of such systems of records. In Germany and Czechoslovakia the records have been used to identify people who co-operated with the security police of the old regimes. In Bulgaria there have been accusations that such information has been released selectively to discredit some politicians. In Germany a system of subject access will be introduced.

This is a selective account of how a few countries are attempting to deal with the problems of asserting rights of personal privacy against a background of state surveillance. For purposes of contrast, it is useful to consider the laws formerly in effect in the Soviet Union. Most of them have been, or are in the process of being changed. The law of what was the Soviet Union also illustrates, perhaps, that statements of principles can be useless without remedies.

Union of Soviet Socialist Republics

In 1973 the USSR ratified both the UN Covenant on Civil and Political Rights and the Covenant on Economic, Social and Cultural Rights. This commitment to individual rights, including the right to privacy, was characterized by some writers as indicating, along with provisions of the 1977 Constitution, a shift in Soviet legal theory. One writer commented that the 1977–8 Constitution demonstrated that the theory had 'come to acknowledge that there are certain bounds beyond which a State must not be permitted to extend its power over individuals'. The writer went on to say:

> The 1977–8 Constitutions contain language without parallel in earlier constitutions reflective of this type of concern: respect for the individual and the protection of rights and freedoms of citizens shall be the duty of all State agencies, social organizations, and officials; citizens have the right to appeal against the actions of officials and of State and social agencies; State and social organizations are obliged to observe the USSR Constitution and Soviet laws; among others.[165]

The right to privacy was guaranteed by the words of Article 56 of the 1977 federal Constitution, together with specific provisions regarding correspondence and telephone communications: 'The privacy of citizens, of correspondence, telephone conversations and telegraphic messages shall be protected by law.'[166] This language was echoed in the constitution of at least one of the Republics, in Article 54 of the 1978 Constitution of the Russian Soviet Federal Socialist Republic (RSFSR): 'The private life of citizens and the secrecy of correspondence, telephone conversations, and telegraph messages are protected by law.'[167]

Although this promise did not result in data protection legislation, there were some specific privacy protection provisions in the criminal code of the RSFSR, Article 135 of which was about 'Violation of the Secrecy of Correspondence': 'The violation of the secrecy of citizens' correspondence shall be punished by correctional tasks for a term not exceeding six months, or by a fine not exceeding 30 roubles, or by social censure.'[168] Article 136 could be seen as a provision to protect physical privacy, providing penalties, including dismissal from office, for 'Violation of Inviolability of Citizens' Dwelling Space'.

Such constitutional and statutory rights were linked with the related duties of citizens in socialist legality. Article 59 of the federal constitution of 1977 said that 'Exercise of rights and freedoms shall be inseparable from performance by citizens of their duties.' The Criminal Code of the RSFSR also included offences such as those of 'Anti-Soviet Agitation and Propaganda' under Article 70, which penalized acts such as 'slanderous fabrications which defame the Soviet state and social system'.[169] Although the privacy of telephone conversations was guaranteed by the federal and republican constitutions, the use of the telephone was subject to administrative rules as well as the criminal law. In an article entitled 'Your Telephone' in *Izvestia*[170] the Honoured Jurist of the RSFSR, K. Budaeva, explained the regulations for the use of telephones approved by the USSR Ministry of Communications. Subscribers were not to permit unauthorized installations and had to keep the telephone in good condition. 'The telephone may not be used for purposes contrary to the interests of the State and social structure. In the event that the subscriber violates these conditions the communications enterprise has the right to disconnect the telephone and remove it.'

The protection of privacy in Article 54 of the RSFSR Constitution was also qualified by the duties of citizens. Article 37 of that constitution provided that 'in exercising their rights and freedoms, citizens may not injure the interests of society and the state or the rights of other citizens'.[171] Article 60 added that 'The citizen of the RSFSR is bound to safeguard the interests of the Soviet state and to promote the growth of its power and authority.'[172]

One particular aspect of information privacy in some Western European countries which has caused public concern is the requirement of passports and the information provided in them about individuals. (Passports are also, of course, bound up with the right to travel within and between countries.) The passport required of every citizen of the USSR was more of an identity card than an accoutrement of international travel.

1. The passport of a citizen of the USSR is the basic document establishing a Soviet citizen's identity. Every USSR citizen of 16 years of age must have a USSR passport.

2. The following information on the identity of a citizen shall be entered in the passport: name, date and place of birth, ethnic origin. The entry on ethnic origin in the passport shall be made on the basis of the ethnic origin of the parents. If the parents have different ethnic origins, then on issuance of the first passport the ethnic origin of either the father or the mother shall be entered, depending on the wish of the recipient of the passport. The entry cannot be changed at a later time. The passport shall also contain the following information on children: name, date, place of birth. This entry shall be made by the Agency for Registering Acts of Civil Status.

4. Notations shall be placed in the passports of citizens: on marriage and divorce, by the Agencies for Registering Acts of Civil Status; on military service by the military commissariats; on registration or deregistration of domicile by the agencies of internal affairs and persons authorized to do so by the Executive Committee of village and hamlet Soviets of working people's deputies.

22. Citizens shall be registered at their place of residence ...

23. Citizens changing their place of residence, and also leaving for another place for temporary residence for more than one and a half months, except those leaving on an official business trip, on vacation, for recreational occupancy of a cottage, for rest or a health cure, must register before leaving. Citizens who do not have in their passports or in other documents provided for in Article 2 of the present Statute a notice of registration may not be registered on arrival elsewhere.[173]

The dismantling of such a system is only part of the process of democratization. The republics of what was the Soviet Union must, as part of the process of creating law-ruled states, adopt measures to implement principles such as those of the Council of Europe's Data Protection Convention. In this they may be assisted by the United Nations' statement of principles of data protection. Unless they become members of the Council of Europe, or are permitted to do so by the Committee of Ministers of the Council, they cannot become party to the Data Protection Convention. But other Eastern European countries are now in the process of becoming members of the Council of Europe and parties to the European Convention on Human Rights with the right of individual petition under Article 25. Hungary and the Czech and Slovak Republics are now in the process of doing this, and may soon become parties to the Data Protection Convention. Poland seems likely to follow soon. Many of the complaints to the Polish Commissioner for Civil Rights Protection would be classified as data protection complaints in countries with such legislation.[174]

In April 1990 the Hungarian government was host to a conference on data protection chaired by Spiros Simitis, the first data protection commissioner in the world, in the *Land* of Hessen (until his retirement in 1991). One contribution was a report that in 1989 the Constitution of Slovenia, then one of the federal republics of Yugoslavia, had amended its constitution to provide that: 'The right to data privacy is guaranteed. The law regulates collecting, processing and purpose of use of personal data. Any use of personal data in a way incompatible with a specialized and lawful purpose is forbidden.' This was followed by a Slovenian Data Protection Act adopted in 1990 which gave effect to the OECD Guidelines and the principles of the Council of Europe Convention. Both a regulatory agency and a parliamentary supervisory committee have been established to implement the Act.

Other new constitutions of Eastern Europe assert the principle of personal privacy. One of the more interesting developments has been a ruling by the Constitutional Court of Hungary on the use of the personal identification number.

Hungary

Article 59 of the Hungarian Constitution adopted in October 1989 provides that: 'In the Hungarian Republic everybody has the right to have his or her personal data protected.' Article 61 further provides that: 'It is everybody's right to have access to public data, and to propagate them.'

These principles are the foundation for the data protection and freedom of information bill introduced in the Hungarian Parliament at the end of 1991. It is interesting that Hungary is apparently the only country apart from Canada to legislate on both these related subjects at the same time. The bill reflects both the OECD Guidelines and Council of Europe Convention principles, and also the Council of Europe Recommendations on access to information held by public authorities.[175]

The Hungarian bill applies to both natural and legal persons, as do a minority of the data protection statutes in Western Europe. The implementation is by a Data Protection Commissioner elected by Parliament on the recommendation of the President, with a National Data Protection Register similar to those in Western Europe. The Commissioner has the power to initiate legal action, and data subjects themselves can also take direct legal action.

While legislation is pending, the Constitutional Court of Hungary has applied Article 59 to rule that the unrestricted use of personal identification numbers is unconstitutional. The Court ruled that one Law Decree and two Cabinet Decrees were null and void and must be repealed by 31 December 1991, except in revised and limited form. The main objections to the laws were that they did not define the purpose for which the information could be used, and that the personal identification number was a means of constructing databases and collecting information from different registers. The Court referred to developments in the United States, France, and Germany, and concluded that the formation of a 'profile of personality' unknown to the data subject was 'particularly prejudicial to the rights of personality'. The Court also referred to Section 35 of the Portuguese Constitution, adopted after the fall of the dictatorship, to the judgment of the German Constitutional Court in the Census case, and to restrictions on the use of the social security number in Canada, among other comparative legal developments, and concluded that: 'the universal personal identification number is, by its essence, contrary to the right of self-government in respect of information. Therefore, only identification numbers which serve a restricted use and a definite purpose are in compliance with the Constitution'. The ruling was delayed until the end of the year to allow public authorities a period of transition, but annulled immediately any requirement for the production of a personal identification number as a condition of exercising any right.[176]

Other Socialist Countries

China

The period of relaxation in China during the 1980s never extended to data protection legislation, although the Chinese criminal code which went into effect in 1980 recognizes information privacy in one sense by Article 149: 'Where a person infringes on a citizen's right of freedom of communication by concealing, destroying or unlawfully opening another's letter, a serious offender shall be sentenced either to fixed-term imprisonment for not more than one year or detention.'[177] A similar provision in Article 191 provides harsher punishment for officials who do the same thing: 'A postal or telecommunication official who, without authorization, secretly opens, conceals, destroys, or discards a letter or telegram shall be sentenced to either fixed-term imprisonment for not more than two years or detention.'

A more interesting aspect of the Chinese code relating to information privacy is the codification of a punishment called 'public surveillance', which is described by the translator as 'uniquely Chinese'.[178]

It is a punishment whereby the offender is subject to labour reform under the control of state organs and mass supervision. The purpose of putting petty offenders under mass surveillance seems to be to reform socially desirable [*sic*] persons. Terms of public surveillance are from three months to two years. During this period, an offender must regularly report his activities to the public security organ. He must apply for permission to change his residence or leave the locality. An offender under public surveillance shall receive the same pay as others doing the same work while engaging in collective productive labour or other work.

To give some idea of the place of such a penalty in the range of possible penalties, Article 36 provides that two days under surveillance shall be calculated as one day in custody. Although it is not classified under 'misconduct in office', another provision, Article 144, seems to contemplate that officials and others may commit offences of interfering with a person's privacy, including the method of putting him under surveillance: 'A person who unlawfully puts another under public surveillance, conducts unlawful search of another's body or illegally intrudes upon a human habitation shall be sentenced to either fixed-term imprisonment for not more than three years or detention.'

Notes

1   *Datalagen* 1973.
2   Freedom of the Press Act (*Tryckfrihetsforordning*) 1766 ; cf. US Freedom of Information Act of 1966 (5 USC 552).
3   11 *Scandinavian Studies in Law* 211 (1967).
4   Secrecy Act, section 7.
5   Drzemczewski, A. (1983), *European Human Rights Convention in Domestic Law*, pp. 124–9, 304–5, Oxford: Oxford University Press.
6   Discussed in Logdberg, Ake (1967), 'The Right in a Person's Own Likeness', 11 *Scandinavian Studies in Law* 211, at 224–5.
7   Section 6.
8   Holm, Niels Eilschou (1979), in Rowat, D. (ed.), *Administrative Secrecy in Developed Countries*, p. 76, London.
9   Private Registers Act, section 1; Public Authorities Registers Act, section 1; the explanation seems to be the pre-existing right of access to manual files as part of the general right.
10 Act No. 69 of 19 June 1970 concerning Public Access to Administrative Documents, amended by Act No. 47 of 11 June 1982.
11 Act No. 48 of 9 June 1978. An authorized English translation is in OECD document DSTI/ICCP/79.11/14.
12 Drzemczewski, op. cit., pp. 131–5, 309–11.
13 Rt. 1952, s. 1217.
14 *Melvin v. Reid*, 112 Cal. App. 285, 297 P. 291 (1931).
15 *Offentlighetsloven: En Kort Orientering* (1971).
16 Section 10.
17 Paper presented by Arve Foyen to Council of Europe conference on data protection, Rome, 1982.

18   *Transnational Data Report*, Vol. VII, No. 7 (October/November 1984), p. 396.
19   Section 17.
20   Section 18.
21   *JO's berättelse* 1966, p. 56.
22   Section 20.
23   Decree, section 1(9).
24   *Transnational Data Report*, Vol. VI, No. 7 (October/November 1983), p. 359.
25   See Drzemczewski, op. cit., pp. 289–95.
26   *Transnational Data Report*, Vol. VIII, No. 4 (June 1985), p. 187.
27   Article 1(1).
28   Article 4(a) and (b).
29   Article 4(d), 4(f) and (g), 4(e).
30   Article 4(h) and (i).
31   Article 5(1).
32   Gallouedec-Genuys, Françoise and Maisl, Herbert (1976), *Le Secret des Fichiers*, Paris: Editions Cujas.
33   Articles 22, 22.
34   *Transnational Data Report*, Vol. VIII, No. 5 (July/August 1985), p. 245.
35   Commission d'Accès, 1980, p. 50, and 1982, p. 28.
36   Commission d'Accès, 1982, pp. 23–4.
37   Deciding on commercial confidentiality claims is an increasing, and increasingly difficult, part of the CADA's workload (Commission d'Accès, 1982, p. 37).
38   Commission d'Accès, 1980, p. 46, 78, 47.
39   See Auburn, F.M. (1974), 'Report of the Sub-Committee of the Law Revision Commission on Computer Data Banks and Privacy', 6 *New Zealand Universities Law Review* 194, October.
40   Section 15.
41   Section 28.
42   Section 2.
43   Section 2(e)(1), (f), and (h).
44   McBride, T. (1984), 'The Official Information Act 1982', *New Zealand Universities Law Review*, Vol. II, pp. 82–9.
45   Danks Committee Supplementary Report, p. 62, 1981.
46   Section 2(1).
47   Section 2.
48   Section 2(12).
49   Section 2.
50   Section 24(5).
51   Sections 27(1)(e), 6(c) and 27(1)(f).
52   Sections 27(1)(e), 27(1)(d).
53   Section 27(1)(g).
54   Section 26(1)(c).
55   *New Zealand Herald*, 17 January 1984.
56   Section 26(1)(b).
57   Section 35.
58   Sections 31(a) and 31(b).
59   Section 32(2).
60   See McBride, op. cit.
61   Sections 35(2) and 35(4).
62   Sections 38(6)(b) and 38(7).
63   Section 34.
64   McBride, op. cit., pp. 99–100, 102.

65   British Columbia Privacy Act 1968, Manitoba Privacy Act 1970, Saskatchewan Privacy Act 1974.
66   Such as nuisance in *Motherwell* v. *Motherwell* (1976), 73 DLR (3d) 62 (Alberta); see Burns (1976), 'Law and Privacy: the Canadian Experience', 54 *Canadian Bar Review* 1.
67   Sections 5, 6, 7, and 8.
68   Section 11, Privacy Act.
69   Section 4(1).
70   Sections 3 and 4(3).
71   Section 13(2).
72   Sections 14, 15(1), 15(2).
73   Section 16.
74   Section 16(3).
75   Section 17.
76   Section 23.
77   Sections 19, 20.
78   Section 54.
79   Annual Report 1984–5, p. 20.
80   Ibid., p. 22.
81   Ibid., p. 23.
82   Ibid., p. 30.
83   Ibid., p. 34.
84   Protection of Privacy Act 1973, section 178.
85   Watt, D. (1979), *Law of Electronic Surveillance in Canada*.
86   *International Social Science Journal*, Vol. XXIV, No. 3, 1972, p. 452.
87   381 US 479 (1965).
88   410 US 113 (1973).
89   5 USC 552a(f)(3).
90   450 F.2d 670 (D.C. Cir. 1971).
91   502 F.2d 133 (3d Cir. 1974).
92   *The File*, 1984.
93   *Department of the Air Force* v. *Rose*, 425 US at 378–9.
94   5 USC 552a(a)(2).
95   The Office of Management and Budget Guidelines make the distinction and say that individuals acting in an entrepreneurial capacity are not covered (at 28951). One district court has agreed; three have not.
96   See p. 44 for discussion of the effect of such an order on transborder data flows.
97   *Victoria Park Racing Grounds* v. *Taylor* (1937) 58 CLR 479, at 495, 'No authority was cited which shows that any general right of privacy exists.'; for a somewhat similar English case, with the same result, see *Bernstein* v. *Skyways* [1978] Q.B. 479.
98   'Unfair Publication: Defamation and Privacy', 130 (Discussion Paper No. 11, 1979), 'Privacy and Intrusions', 96 (Discussion Paper No. 13, 1980), 'Privacy and Personal Information', 122 (Discussion Paper No. 14, 1980); and see 'The Computer, the Individual, and the Law', 55 *Australian Law Journal* 443 (1981) by Mr Justice Kirby of the Law Reform Commission.
99   Victoria Listening Devices Act 1969, New South Wales Listening Devices Act 1969, and Queensland Invasion of Privacy Act 1971.
100   *Transnational Data Report*, Vol. VII, No. 2 (March 1984), p. 61.
101   Sections 11, 19(1)(b), and 48.
102   Sections 12(2) and 12(2)(a).
103   Section 7(1) and Schedule 1.
104   Section 33(1)(a)(i)(ii), and 33(1)(a)(iii), (1)(b).

105 Section 33(1)(a)(iv), and 33(1)(b).
106 Section 41(3).
107 Sections 38, 42, and 46.
108 [1983] *Europäische Grundrechte Zeitschrift* 577; English translation in *Human Rights Journal*, Vol. 5, No. 1, pp. 94–116.
109 Decision of 16 July 1969, 27 *Entscheidungen des Bundesverfassunsgerichts* 1.
110 Oliver and von Borries in *Public Law*, 1984, p. 203.
111 Nos 73/403 and 81/1059.
112 *Public Law*, 1984, p. 205.
113 Section 39(1).
114 Sections 12(2), 19(4).
115 Section 13.
116 Section 13(3)(1), (2), and (3).
117 Section 13(3)(3).
118 Sections 26(1) and 34(1), 28(1) and 38, 30 and 40.
119 *Transnational Data Report*, Vol. V, No. 6 (September 1982), p. 269.
120 XXIII *Pasicrisie Luxembourgeoise*, (1975–7), 182–9.
121 *Journal des Tribunaux*, (1980), 489–92, at 491.
122 No. 6/80, 20 November 1980 (registry No. 418).
123 Article 15(b).
124 Article 18.
125 Article 11.
126 *Transnational Data Report*, Vol. VII, No. 7 (October/November 1984), pp. 388–90.
127 Lord Kilbrandon (1971), 'The Law of Privacy in Scotland', 2 *Cambrian Law Review* 35.
128 The subject access provision does not distinguish between manual and automated records, and it is limited to records kept on natural persons. It does, however, distinguish between those seeking credit for personal use (section 159) and those seeking credit for business purposes (section 160). The right of those seeking business credit is more restricted. Compare the US Privacy Act distinction between individuals and 'entrepreneurial' individuals (pp. 87–8).
129 Section 158(5).
130 *Computers and Privacy* (Cmnd. 6353), para. 31.
131 Home Affairs Committee, First Report, Annual Report of the Data Protection Registrar with Proceedings of the Committee and Minutes of Evidence, HC 115, 12 December 1990.
132 Speech by the Rt. Hon. David Waddington, Minister of State, Home Office, Toronto, May 1984.
133 *Malone v. Metropolitan Police Commissioner* [1979] 3 All E.R. 620.
134 *Breach of Confidence*, Law Commission Report No. 110, October 1981 (Cmnd. 8388).
135 Para. 6.35.
136 Para. 6.37.
137 Para. 7.2(24)(iii).
138 Para 7.2(24)(v).
139 Para. 6.35, noting that aerial photographs had been allowed in *Bernstein v. Skyviews* [1978] Q.B. 479.
140 For an explanation of how the Convention was thought to have been given constitutional status, but was determined by the Constitutional Court not to have it, and was then given it with retroactive effect, see Drzemczewski, A. (1983), *European Human Rights Convention in Domestic Law*, pp. 93–8, Oxford: Oxford University Press.
141 Article 1, section 1.

142   See Pagano, R. (1982), *Panorama of Personal Data Protection Laws*, p.3, Rome: Camera dei Deputati; and references to Hogrebe, E. (1981), 'Les personnes morales dans les législations européennes en matière de protection des données', Paris: OECD.

143   Section 28.

144   *X. v. Iceland*, application 6825/74, 19 *Yearbook* (1976), 342–72.

145   Report of the Committee on Privacy, Cmnd 5012, Appendix 1, Table H, p. 238.

146   *Transnational Data Report*, Vol. VIII, No. 2 (March 1985), pp. 68–9.

147   28 *Laws of Israel* 97 (incorporated as section 2(6) of the Protection of Privacy Law).

148   See Gavison, Ellman (1977), in 12 *Israel Law Review* 155, 172.

149   33 *Laws of the State of Israel* 141.

150   Section 18(3).

151   Section 18(2) (b).

152   Section 20.

153   Sections 4, 29.

154   Section 5.

155   Section 34.

156   Sections 7–17.

157   See Segal, Z. (1982), 'A General Right to Privacy: the Israeli *v.* the English Approach', *Public Law* 240.

158   Thomashausen, A. (1980), 'Basic Rights, Liberty, and their Protection under the New Portugese Constitution of 1976', *Human Rights Law Journal*, Vol. 1, Nos 1–4, pp. 182–208, at 192; English translation, pp. 416–29.

159   Article 41.

160   Section 13.

161   Law No. 1599/1986.

162   'Opinion 584/87 by Public Administration Counsel X. Papahristou.'

163   Law No. 1599/1986.

164   Article 2, para. 4.

165   Butler, W. E. (1983), *Soviet Law*, p. 144, London: Butterworths.

166   English translation in Hazard, J., Butler, W.E., and Maggs, P. (eds) (1977), *The Soviet Legal System* (3d ed.), p. 603, New York: Oceana Publications. Whatever the present state of information privacy under Soviet law, its constitutional recognition is not a new development of the 1970s. Article 128 of the 1936 Constitution already provided that: 'The inviolability of homes of citizens and privacy of correspondence are protected by law.'

167   Simons, W.B. (ed.) (1980), *The Soviet Codes of Law*, p. 19, Amsterdam: Sijthoff & Noordhoff.

168   *The Soviet Codes of Law*, p. 100.

169   *The Soviet Codes of Law*, p. 93.

170   29 March 1975, p. 5; quoted in *The Soviet State and its Citizens*, pp. 103–4.

171   *The Soviet Codes of Law*, p. 15.

172   *The Soviet Codes of Law*, p. 20.

173   Statute on the Passport System in the USSR, 28 August 1984 [1974], *Vedomosti Verkhovnogo Sovieta SSSR*, No. 19, item 109; in *The Soviet State and its Citizens*, p. 95.

174   Mednis, Arwid (1990), 'DP-Related Cases in Poland', *Transnational Data Report Hungary*, Special Issue, pp. 28–9.

175   Recommendation No. 854 (1979) of the Parliamentary Assembly of the Council of Europe to Member States on Access by the Public to Government Records and Freedom of Information, and Recommendation No. R(81) 19 of the Committee of Ministers of the Council of Europe to Member States on Access to Information held by Public Authorities.

176 Decision in File No. 983/B/1990/3 of 9 April 1991.
177 Chin Kim (trans.) (1982), *The Criminal Code of the People's Republic of China*, pp. 63–4, London: Sweet & Maxwell.
178 Ibid., p. 7.

4 Conclusions

The 1972 study divided the protection of privacy into two questions: what are acceptable methods of surveillance or inquiry into the private lives of individuals, and in what circumstances and subject to what safeguards is it proper to collect, disseminate or publish information about a person's private life? After setting out several conclusions, the report commented that 'the latest and potentially the greatest threat to privacy is the recording, storing, and dissemination of personal information by computers'. From the considerations developed in the present study, several new conclusions may be drawn.

The first may justify a degree of qualified optimism: since 1972 the spread of automated information handling has been very nearly matched by the spread of legislation to protect the privacy of individuals from the threats of such automation. The original subnational data protection law in Hessen has now been followed by 18 national laws, with at least another six countries hovering on the brink of legislation. This trend must be welcomed by anyone concerned with human rights.

In those of the developed countries where increasing computerization has given rise to real fears of violations of the accepted bounds of the privacy of the ordinary citizen, governments have in fact moved to counteract these threats (even where they have emanated from their own operations) by enacting data protection laws. The pressures on them have come from a variety of sources: powerful lobbying by groups concerned with the maintenance of civil liberties, amplified by the press; increasing public concern, persuading politicians that votes might hang on their attitudes to such laws; and also pressures from the business community, concerned not to risk a serious throttling of its transnational data flows. In the United Kingdom in the early 1980s, for example, support for data protection came from a wide *ad hoc* alliance of interests, including (for different reasons) industrialists, trade unions, government departments, the liberal professions, civil libertarians, consumerists, and the press. In the end, the only remaining opponents were the Home Office and the mail-order industry. Concern for privacy seems to cross most political, economic and social divisions.

It therefore seems possible that technological threats of this kind are capable of generating their own specific immune responses, provided that the underlying condition of the social organism is sufficiently healthy. It also seems as if the necessary immunological conditions do in fact exist in the kinds of developed and traditionally democratic societies in which modern technology also finds its most fertile ground.

The question then arises whether the development of technology is a necessary precondition for the development of protective measures such as the data protection laws which are now becoming a common standard within the member nations of the Council of Europe, the EC, and the OECD. Clearly, in countries where large-scale computerization is still far over the horizon, public resources could be much better deployed in the short term than by installing data protection laws whose effects are likely to remain theoretical for years, if not for decades. And yet there may be a case for installing a regulatory regime before the technology arrives, precisely in order to become more receptive to it, and less at risk from being shut out from its introduction or development by failing to join the appropriate club, currently represented by the States Parties to the Council of Europe's Data Protection Convention, but open to accession by any other state that is willing to comply with its provisions.

A second, and perhaps more tentative, conclusion is that the specific threat of data surveillance, and the welcome but equally specific response of data protection, only exemplify a more general phenomenon. This has to do with the nature and functions of information in human society, a subject still lacking the degree of study that one would expect, considering its obvious importance to mankind as a whole, and its future development on this planet. As needs for essential material goods gradually become satisfied, more of the development in which so much effort is now invested will depend for its realization on a plentiful and unrestricted flow of information.

Here, perhaps, is the most ill defined, and yet potentially the most acute, of the problems which are beginning to become apparent in this entire area. As we have noticed earlier (see the Introduction above), information behaves in some respects like one of the familiar tangible commodities, and yet in other respects defies their laws. Unlike, say, copper or cocoa, it can be reproduced almost infinitely at minimal cost. It may be taken for profit without depriving anyone of anything, other than his or her previously exclusive possession of it, which may have given them a measure of power precisely because others did not share it with them. And yet it may cost a great deal to create in the first place, and without the expectation of an adequate reward there would be few incentives to encourage that creation. Both the promotion of free flow, and its social regulation, may therefore present quite different problems in the case of information from those which are familiar in the case of tangible commodities.

In at least one respect, however, information flows are subject to the familiar problems of markets. If a market is totally free, it will (necessarily) promote the interests of those who are sufficiently rich, or knowledgeable, or with the foresight to know how to manipulate it for their benefit, and gradually exclude the weak or inefficient from any share in its benefits. Yet total control of markets is now also known to be ineffective, stultifying their operations and in the end doing no more than to drive them underground. Finding the most appropriate point of balance between these two extremes is a problem which continues to occupy the time of economists and politicians of all political and ideological preconceptions. And perhaps the problem is even greater where the 'commodity' concerned is at one and the same time as crucial, and yet so far as little studied, as information.

The communication of information is very often both the exercise of a human right and an economic activity. The ability to control at least some information about oneself is at the very core of personal identity and political autonomy, and the interactive disclosure of that information is the currency of society. But the buying and selling and trading of that information is increasingly important both as economic activity and means of political control. Developments in information technology have raised the stakes, both risks and benefits, in all these transactions so dramatically as to seem altogether different in kind.[1] Yet the principles of international human rights law, derived from centuries-old values, still apply, from the decision of the Hungarian Constitutional Court to principles of the United Nations.

Note

1   See, for example, Sieghart, P. (1977), 'Computers, Information, Privacy and the Law', *Journal of the Royal Society of Arts*, Vol. CXXV, No. 5252, pp. 456–72, July; 'Information, Technology, Law and Human Rights', *Review of the International Commission of Jurists*, June 1981; 'Towards a General Declaration on Transborder Data Flows', Report to OECD, 1983 (unpublished); and Michael, J. (1986), 'The Case for Information Law', in *New Communication Technology and the Public Interest: comparative perspectives on policy and research*, London: Sage.

APPENDICES

APPENDICES

Appendix 1: OECD Guidelines Governing the Protection of Privacy and Transborder Flows of Personal Data

RECOMMENDATION OF THE COUNCIL OF EUROPE ADOPTED AT ITS 523RD MEETING ON 23 SEPTEMBER 1980*

The Council,

Having regard to Articles 1(c), 3(a) and 5(b) of the Convention of the Organization for Economic Cooperation and Development of 14 December 1960;

Recognizing:
– that, although national laws and policies may differ, member countries have a common interest in protecting privacy and individual liberties, and in reconciling fundamental but competing values such as privacy and the free flow of information;
– that automatic processing and transborder flows of personal data create new forms of relationship among countries and require the development of compatible rules and practices;
– that transborder flows of personal data contribute to economic and social development;
– that domestic legislation concerning privacy protection and transborder flows of personal data may hinder such transborder flows;

Determined to advance the free flow of information between member countries and to avoid the creation of unjustified obstacles to the development of economic and social relations among member countries;

*The Australian, Canadian, Irish, Turkish and United Kingdom Governments abstained.

RECOMMENDS

1   That member countries take into account in their domestic legislation the principles concerning the protection of privacy and individual liberties set forth in the Guidelines contained in the Annex to
this Recommendation which is an integral part thereof;

2   That member countries endeavour to remove or avoid creating,
in the name of privacy protection, unjustified obstacles to transborder
flows of personal data;

3   That member countries cooperate in the implementation of the
Guidelines set forth in the Annex;

4   That member countries agree as soon as possible on specific procedures of consultation and cooperation for the application of these
Guidelines.

Annex

PART ONE – GENERAL

Definitions
1   For the purposes of these Guidelines:
(a)   'data controller' means a party who, according to domestic law,
is competent to decide about the contents and use of personal data
regardless of whether or not such data are collected, stored, processed or disseminated by that party or by an agent on its behalf;
(b)   'personal data' means any information relating to an identified
or identifiable individual (data subject);
(c)   'transborder flows of personal data' means movements of personal data across national borders.

Scope of Guidelines
2   These Guidelines apply to personal data, whether in the public or
private sectors, which, because of the manner in which they are
processed, or because of their nature or the context in which they are
used, pose a danger to privacy and individual liberties.

3   These Guidelines should not be interpreted as preventing:
(a)   the application, to different categories of personal data, of different protective measures depending upon their nature and the context in which they are collected, stored, processed or disseminated;

(b) the exclusion from the application of the Guidelines of personal data which obviously do not contain any risk to privacy and individual liberties: or
(c) the application of the Guidelines only to automatic processing of personal data.

4 Exceptions to the Principles contained in Parts Two and Three of these Guidelines, including those relating to national sovereignty, national security and public policy (*ordre public*), should be:
(a) as few as possible, and
(b) made known to the public.

5 In the particular case of Federal countries the observance of these Guidelines may be affected by the division of powers in the Federation.

6 These Guidelines should be regarded as minimum standards which are capable of being supplemented by additional measures for the protection of privacy and individual liberties.

PART TWO – BASIC PRINCIPLES OF NATIONAL APPLICATION

Collection limitation principle
7 There should be limits to the collection of personal data and any such data should be obtained by lawful and fair means and, where appropriate, with the knowledge or consent of the data subject.

Data quality principle
8 Personal data should be relevant to the purposes for which they are to be used, and, to the extent necessary for those purposes, should be accurate, complete and kept up-to-date.

Purpose specification principle
9 The purposes for which personal data are collected should be specified not later than at the time of data collection and the subsequent use limited to the fulfilment of those purposes or such others as are not incompatible with those purposes and as are specified on each occasion of change of purpose.

Use limitation principle
10 Personal data should not be disclosed, made available or otherwise used for purposes other than those specified in accordance with Paragraph 9 except:
(a) with the consent of the data subject; or
(b) by the authority of law.

Security safeguards principle
11   Personal data should be protected by reasonable security safeguards against such risks as loss or unauthorized access, destruction, use, modification or disclosure of data.

Openness principle
12   There should be a general policy of openness about developments, practices and policies with respect to personal data. Means should be readily available of establishing the existence and nature of personal data, and the main purposes of their use, as well as the identity and usual residence of the data controller.

Individual participation principle
13   An individual should have the right:
(a)   to obtain from a data controller, or otherwise, confirmation of whether or not the data controller has data relating to him;
(b)   to have communicated to him, data relating to him
i)   within a reasonable time;
ii)   at a charge, if any, that is not excessive;
iii)   in a reasonable manner; and
iv)   in a form that is readily intelligible to him;
(c)   to be given reasons if a request made under sub-paragraphs (a) and (b) is denied, and to be able to challenge such denial; and
(d)   to challenge data relating to him and, if the challenge is successful, to have the data erased, rectified, completed or amended.

Accountability principle
14   A data controller should be accountable for complying with measures which give effect to the principles stated above.

PART THREE – BASIC PRINCIPLES OF INTERNATIONAL APPLICATION: FREE FLOW AND LEGITIMATE RESTRICTIONS

15   Member countries should take into consideration the implications for other member countries of domestic processing and re-export of personal data.

16   Member countries should take all reasonable and appropriate steps to ensure that transborder flows of personal data, including transit through a member country, are uninterrupted and secure.

17   A member country should refrain from restricting transborder flows of personal data between itself and another member country except where the latter does not yet substantially observe these Guidelines or where the re-export of such data would circumvent its

domestic privacy legislation. A member country may also impose restrictions in respect of certain categories of personal data for which its domestic privacy legislation includes specific regulations in view of the nature of those data and for which the other member country provides no equivalent protection.

18   Member countries should avoid developing laws, policies and practices in the name of the protection of privacy and individual liberties, which would create obstacles to transborder flows of personal data that would exceed requirements for such protection.

PART FOUR – NATIONAL IMPLEMENTATION

19   In implementing domestically the principles set forth in Parts Two and Three, member countries should establish legal, administrative or other procedures or institutions for the protection of privacy and individual liberties in respect of personal data. Member countries should in particular endeavour to :
(a)   adopt appropriate domestic legislation;
(b)   encourage and support self-regulation, whether in the form of codes of conduct or otherwise;
(c)   provide for reasonable means for individuals to exercise their rights;
(d)   provide for adequate sanctions and remedies in case of failures to comply with measures which implement the principles set forth in Parts Two and Three; and
(e)   ensure that there is no unfair discrimination against data subjects .

PART FIVE – INTERNATIONAL COOPERATION

20   Member countries should, where requested, make known to other member countries details of the observance of the principles set forth in these Guidelines. Member countries should also ensure that procedures for transborder flows of personal data and for the protection of privacy and individual liberties are simple and compatible with those of other member countries which comply with these Guidelines.

21   Member countries should establish procedures to facilitate:
(a)   information exchange related to these Guidelines; and
(b)   mutual assistance in the procedural and investigative matters involved.

22 Member countries should work towards the development of principles, domestic and international, to govern the applicable law in the case of transborder flows of personal data.

Appendix 2: Council of Europe Convention for the Protection of Individuals with regard to Automatic Processing of Personal Data

FINAL DRAFT APPROVED BY EUROPEAN COMMITTEE ON LEGAL COOPERATION, 27 JUNE 1980 AND PRESENTED TO COUNCIL OF MINISTERS FOR ADOPTION

PREAMBLE

The Member States of the Council of Europe, signatory hereto,

Considering that the aim of the Council of Europe is to achieve greater unity between its Members, based in particular on respect for the rule of law, as well as human rights and fundamental freedoms,

Considering that it is desirable to extend the safeguards for everyone's rights and fundamental freedoms, and in particular the right to respect for privacy, taking account of the increasing flow across frontiers of personal data undergoing automatic processing,

Reaffirming at the same time their commitment to freedom of information regardless of frontiers,

Recognizing that it is necessary to reconcile the fundamental values of the respect for privacy and the free flow of information between peoples,

Have agreed as follows:

CHAPTER I – GENERAL PROVISIONS

Article 1 – Object and purpose
The purpose of this Convention is to secure in the territory of each Party for every individual, whatever his nationality or residence, respect for his rights and fundamental freedoms, and in particular his right to privacy, with regard to automatic processing of personal data relating to him ('data protection').

Article 2 – Definitions
For the purpose of this Convention:
(a)   'personal data' means any information relating to an identified or identifiable individual ('data subject');
(b)   'automated data file' means any set of data undergoing automatic processing;
(c)   'automatic processing' includes the following operations if carried out in whole or in part by automated means: storage of data; carrying out of logical and/or arithmetical operations on those data; their alteration, erasure, retrieval or dissemination;
(d)   'controller of the file' means the natural or legal person, public authority, agency or any other body who is competent according to his national law to decide what should be the purpose of the automated data file, which categories of personal data should be stored and which processes should be applied to them.

Article 3 – Scope
1   The Parties undertake to apply this Convention to automated personal data files and automatic processing of personal data in the public and private sectors.
2   Any State may, at the time of signature or when depositing its instrument of ratification, acceptance, approval or accession, or at any later time, give notice by a declaration addressed to the Secretary General of the Council of Europe:
(a)   that it will not apply this Convention to certain categories of automated personal data files, a list of which will be deposited. In this list it shall not include, however, categories of automated data files subject in its domestic law to data protection provisions. Consequently, it shall amend this list by a new declaration whenever additional categories of automated personal data files are subjected to data protection provisions in its domestic law;
(b)   that it will apply this Convention also to information relating to groups of persons, associations, foundations, companies, corporations and any other bodies consisting directly or indirectly of individuals, whether or not such bodies possess legal personality;

(c) that it will apply this Convention also to personal data files which are not processed automatically.

3 Any State which has extended the scope of the Convention by any of the declarations provided for in sub-paragraph 2(b) or (c) above may give notice in the said declaration that such extensions shall apply only to certain categories of personal data files, a list of which will be deposited.

4 Any Party which has excluded certain categories of automated personal data files by a declaration provided for in subparagraph 2(a) above may not claim the application of this Convention to such categories by a Party which has not excluded them.

5 Likewise, a Party which has not made one or other of the extensions provided for in sub-paragraph 2(b) and (c) above may not claim the application of this Convention on these points with respect to a Party which has made such extensions.

6 The declarations provided for in paragraph 2 above shall take effect from the moment of the entry into force of the Convention with regard to the State which has made them at the time of signature or deposit of its instrument of ratification, acceptance, approval or accession, or three months after their receipt by the Secretary General of the Council of Europe if they have been formulated at any later time. These declarations may be withdrawn, in whole or in part, by a notification addressed to the Secretary General of the Council of Europe. Such withdrawals shall take effect three months after the date of receipt of such notification.

CHAPTER II – BASIC PRINCIPLES FOR DATA PROTECTION

Article 4 – Duties of the Parties
1 Each Party shall take the necessary measures in its domestic law to give effect to the basic principles for data protection set out in this chapter.
2 These measures shall be taken at the latest at the time of entry into force of this Convention in respect of that Party.

Article 5 – Quality of data
Personal data undergoing automatic processing shall be:
(a) obtained and processed fairly and lawfully;
(b) stored for specified and legitimate purposes and not used in a way incompatible with those purposes;
(c) adequate, relevant and not excessive in relation to the purpose for which they are stored;
(d) accurate and, where necessary, kept up-to-date;

(e)   preserved in a form which permits identification of the data subjects for no longer than is required for the purpose for which those data are stored.

Article 6 – Special categories of data
Personal data revealing racial origin, political opinions or religious or other beliefs, as well as personal data concerning health or sexual life, may not be processed automatically unless domestic law provides appropriate safeguards. The same shall apply to personal data relating to criminal convictions.

Article 7 – Data security
Appropriate security measures shall be taken for the protection of personal data stored in automated data files against accidental or unauthorized destruction or accidental loss as well as against unauthorized access, alteration or dissemination.

Article 8 – Additional safeguards for the data subject
Any person shall be enabled:
(a)   to establish the existence of an automated personal data file, its main purposes, as well as the identity and habitual residence or principal place of business of the controller of the file;
(b)   to obtain at reasonable intervals and without excessive delay or expense confirmation of whether personal data relating to him are stored in the automated data file as well as communication to him of such data in an intelligible form;
(c)   to obtain, as the case may be, rectification or erasure of such data if these have been processed contrary to the provisions of domestic law giving effect to the basic principles set out in Articles 5 and 6 of this Convention;
(d)   to have a remedy if a request for confirmation or, as the case may be, communication, rectification or erasure as referred to in paragraphs (b) and (c) of this article is not complied with.

Article 9 – Exceptions and restrictions
1   No exception to the provisions of Articles 5, 6 and 8 of this Convention shall be allowed except within the limits defined in this article.
2   Derogation from the provisions of Articles 5, 6 and 8 of this Convention shall be allowed where such derogation provided for by the law of the Party constitutes a necessary measure in a democratic society in the interests of:
(a)   protecting state security, public safety, the monetary interests of the State or the suppression of criminal offences;
(b)   protecting the data subject or the rights and freedoms of others.

3 Restrictions on the exercise of the rights specified in Article 8, paragraphs (b), (c) and (d) may be provided by law with respect to automated personal data files used for statistics or for scientific research purposes when there is obviously no risk of an infringement of the privacy of the data subjects.

Article 10 – Sanctions and remedies
Each Party undertakes to establish appropriate sanctions and remedies for violations of provisions of domestic law giving effect to the basic principles for data protection set out in this chapter.

Article 11 – Extended protection
None of the provisions of this chapter shall be interpreted as limiting or otherwise affecting the possibility for a Party to grant data subjects a wider measure of protection than that stipulated in this Convention.

CHAPTER III – TRANSBORDER DATA FLOWS

Article 12 – Transborder flows of personal data and domestic law
1 The following provisions shall apply to the transfer across national borders, by whatever medium, of personal data undergoing automatic processing or collected with a view to their being automatically processed.
2 A Party shall not, for the sole purpose of the protection of privacy, prohibit or subject to special authorization transborder flows of personal data going to the territory of another Party.
3 Nevertheless, each Party shall be entitled to derogate from the provisions of paragraph 2:
(a) insofar as its legislation includes specific regulations for certain categories of personal data or of automated personal data files, because of the nature of those data or those files, except where the regulations of the other Party provide an equivalent protection;
(b) when the transfer is made from its territory to the territory of a non-Contracting State through the intermediary of the territory of another Party, in order to avoid such transfers resulting in circumvention of the legislation of the Party referred to at the beginning of this paragraph.

CHAPTER IV – MUTUAL ASSISTANCE

Article 13 – Cooperation between Parties
1 The Parties agree to render each other mutual assistance in order to implement this Convention.
2 For that purpose:

(a)   each Party shall designate one or more authorities the name and address of each of which it shall communicate to the Secretary General of the Council of Europe;
(b)   each Party which has designated more than one authority shall specify in its communication referred to in the previous sub-paragraph the competence of each authority.
3   An authority designated by a Party shall at the request of an authority designated by another Party:
(a)   furnish information on its law and administrative practice in the field of data protection;
(b)   for the sole purpose of protection of privacy, take all appropriate measures, in conformity with its domestic law, for furnishing factual information relating to specific automatic processing carried out in its territory, with the exception however of the personal data being processed.

Article 14 – Assistance to data subjects resident abroad
1   Each Party shall assist any person resident abroad to exercise the rights conferred by its domestic law giving effect to the principles set out in Article 8 of this Convention.
2   When such a person resides in the territory of another Party he shall be given the option of submitting his request through the intermediary of the authority designated by that Party.
3   The request for assistance shall contain all the necessary particulars, relating inter alia to:
(a)   the name, address and any other relevant particulars identifying the person making the request;
(b)   the automated personal data file to which the request pertains, or its controller;
(c)   the nature of the request.

Article 15 – Safeguards concerning assistance rendered by designated authorities
1   An authority designated by a Party which has received information from an authority designated by another Party either accompanying a request for assistance or in reply to its own request for assistance shall not use that information for purposes other than those specified in the request for assistance.
2   Each Party shall see to it that the persons belonging to or acting on behalf of the designated authority shall be bound by appropriate restrictions of secrecy or confidentiality with regard to that information.
3   In no case may a designated authority be allowed to make a request for assistance on behalf of a data subject resident abroad, as

referred to in Article 14, paragraph 2 of its own accord and without the express consent of the person concerned.

Article 16 – Refusal of requests for assistance
A designated authority to which a request for assistance is addressed under Articles 13 or 14 of this Convention may not refuse to comply with it unless:
(a)   the request is not compatible with the powers in the field of data protection of the authorities responsible for replying;
(b)   the request does not comply with the provisions of this Convention;
(c)   compliance with the request would be incompatible with the sovereignty, security or public policy (ordre public) of the Party by which it was designated, or with the rights and fundamental freedoms of persons under the jurisdiction of that Party.

Article 17 – Costs and procedures of assistance
1   Mutual assistance which the Parties render each other under Article 13, and assistance they render to data subjects abroad under Article 14 shall not give rise to the payment of any costs or fees other than those incurred for experts and interpreters. The latter costs or fees shall be borne by the Party which has designated the authority making the request for assistance.
2   The data subject may be charged no costs or fees in connection with the steps taken on his behalf in the territory of another Party other than those lawfully payable by residents of that Party.
3   Other details concerning the assistance relating in particular to the forms and procedures and the languages to be used, shall be established directly between the Parties concerned.

CHAPTER V – CONSULTATIVE COMMITTEE

Article 18 – Composition of the Committee
1   A Consultative Committee shall be set up after the entry into force of this Convention.
2   Each Party shall appoint a representative to the Committee and a deputy representative. Any Member State of the Council of Europe which is not a Party to the Convention shall have the right to be represented on the Committee by an observer.
3   The Consultative Committee may, by unanimous decision, invite any non-Member State of the Council of Europe which is not a Party to the Convention to be represented by an observer at any of its meetings.

Article 19 – Functions of the Committee

The Consultative Committee:

(a)   may make proposals with a view to facilitating or improving the application of the Convention;

(b)   may make proposals for amendment of this Convention in conformity with Article 21;

(c)   shall formulate its opinion on any proposal for amendment of this Convention which is referred to it in conformity with Article 21, paragraph 3;

(d)   may, at the request of a Party, express an opinion on any question concerning the application of this Convention.

Article 20 – Procedure

1   The Consultative Committee shall be convened by the Secretary General of the Council of Europe. Its first meeting shall be held within 12 months of the entry into force of this Convention. It shall subsequently meet at least once every two years and in any case when one third of the representatives of the Parties request its convocation.

2   A majority of representatives of the Parties shall constitute a quorum for a meeting of the Consultative Committee.

3   After each of its meetings, the Consultative Committee shall submit to the Committee of Ministers of the Council of Europe a report on its work and on the functioning of the Convention.

4   Subject to the provisions of this Convention, the Consultative Committee shall draw up its own Rules of Procedure.

CHAPTER VI – AMENDMENTS

Article 21 – Amendments

1   Amendments to this Convention may be proposed by a Party, the Committee of Ministers of the Council of Europe or the Consultative Committee.

2   Any proposal for amendment shall be communicated by the Secretary General of the Council of Europe to the Member States of the Council of Europe and to every non-Member State which has acceded to or has been invited to accede to this Convention in accordance with the provisions of Article 23.

3   Moreover, any amendment proposed by a Party or the Committee of Ministers shall be communicated to the Consultative Committee which shall submit to the Committee of Ministers its opinion on that proposed amendment.

4   The Committee of Ministers shall consider the proposed amendment and any opinion submitted by the Consultative Committee and may approve the amendment.

5 The text of any amendment approved by the Committee of Ministers in accordance with paragraph 4 of this article shall be forwarded to the Parties for acceptance.

6 Any amendment approved in accordance with paragraph 4 of this article shall come into force on the thirtieth day after all Parties have informed the Secretary General of their acceptance thereof.

CHAPTER VII – FINAL CLAUSES

Article 22 – Entry into force

1 This Convention shall be open for signature by the Member States of the Council of Europe. It is subject to ratification, acceptance or approval. Instruments of ratification, acceptance or approval shall be deposited with the Secretary General of the Council of Europe.

2 This Convention shall enter into force on the first day of the month following the expiration of a period of three months after the date on which five Member States of the Council of Europe have expressed their consent to be bound by the Convention in accordance with the provisions of the preceding paragraph.

3 In respect of any Member State which subsequently expresses its consent to be bound by it, the Convention shall enter into force on the first day of the month following the expiration of a period of three months after the date of the deposit of the instrument of ratification, acceptance or approval.

Article 23 – Accession by non-Member States

1 After the entry into force of this Convention, the Committee of Ministers of the Council of Europe may invite any State not a member of the Council of Europe to accede to this Convention by a decision taken by the majority provided by Article 20(d) of the Statute of the Council of Europe and by the unanimous vote of the representatives of the Contracting States entitled to sit on the Committee.

2 In respect of any acceding State, the Convention shall enter into force on the first day of the month following the expiration of a period of three months after the date of deposit of the instrument of ratification with the Secretary General of the Council of Europe.

Article 24 – Territorial clause

1 Any State may at the time of signature or when depositing its instrument of ratification, acceptance, approval or accession, specify the territory or territories to which this Convention shall apply.

2 Any State may at any later date, by a declaration addressed to the Secretary General of the Council of Europe, extend the application of this Convention to any other territory specified in the declaration. In

respect of such territory the Convention shall enter into force on the first day of the month following the expiration of a period of three months after the date of receipt by the Secretary General of such declaration.

3   Any declaration made under the two preceding paragraphs may, in respect of any territory specified in such declaration, be withdrawn by a notification addressed to the Secretary General. The withdrawal shall become effective on the first day of the month following the expiration of a period of six months after the date of receipt of such notification by the Secretary General.

Article 25 – Reservations
No reservation may be made in respect of the provisions of this Convention.

Article 26 – Denunciation
1   Any Party may at any time denounce this Convention by means of a notification addressed to the Secretary General of the Council of Europe.

2   Such denunciation shall become effective on the first day of the month following the expiration of a period of six months after the date of receipt of the notification by the Secretary General.

Article 27 – Notifications
The Secretary General of the Council of Europe shall notify the Member States of the Council and any State which has acceded to this Convention of:

(a)   any signature;

(b)   the deposit of any instrument of ratification, acceptance, approval or accession;

(c)   any date of entry into force of this Convention in accordance with Articles 22, 23 and 24;

(d)   any other act, notification or communication relating to this Convention.

Appendix 3: UN Recommended Guidelines

Human Rights and Scientific and Technological Developments

Revised version of the guidelines for the regulation of computerized personal data files prepared by Mr Louis Joinet, Special Rapporteur

I. Introduction

1. At its forty-fourth session, the General Assembly adopted resolution 44/132, on 15 December 1989, entitled 'Guidelines for the regulation of computerized personal data files' by which it invited the Sub-Commission's special Rapporteur, Mr Louis Joinet, to submit to the Commission, at its forty-sixth session, a revised version of the draft guidelines, taking into account the comments and suggestions submitted by eight Governments (A/44/606 and Add. 1), some of which had supplemented or confirmed the comments communicated earlier to the Special Rapporteur and which he had already taken into consideration.

2. This document, prepared pursuant to General Assembly resolution 44/132, contains the revised version of the guidelines for the regulation of computerized personal data files prepared by the Special Rapporteur, Mr Louis Joinet.

II. Guidelines Concerning Computerized Personal Data Files

The procedures for implementing regulations concerning computerized personal data files are left to the initiative of each State subject to the following orientations:

A.   *Principles concerning the minimum guarantees that should be provided in national legislations*

1.   Principle of Lawfulness and Fairness

Information about persons should not be collected or processed in unfair or unlawful ways, nor should it be used for ends contrary to the purposes and principles of the Charter of the United Nations.

2.   Principle of Accuracy

Persons responsible for the compilation of files or those responsible for keeping them have an obligation to conduct regular checks on the accuracy and relevance of the data recorded and to ensure that they are kept as complete as possible in order to avoid errors of omission and that they are kept up to date regularly or when the information contained in a file is used, as long as they are being processed.

3.   Principle of the Purpose-specification

The purpose which a file is to serve and its utilization in terms of that purpose should be specified, legitimate and, when it is established, receive a certain amount of publicity or be brought to the attention of the person concerned, in order to make it possible subsequently to ensure that:

(a)   All the personal data collected and recorded remain relevant and adequate to the purposes so specified;

(b)   None of the said personal data is used or disclosed, except with the consent of the person concerned, for purposes incompatible with those specified;

(c)   The period for which the personal data are kept does not exceed that which would enable the achievement of the purpose so specified.

4.   Principle of Interested-person Access

Everyone who offers proof of identity has the right to know whether information concerning him is being processed and to obtain it in an intelligible form, without undue delay or expense, and to have appropriate rectifications or erasures made in the case of unlawful, unnecessary or inaccurate entries and, when it is being communicated, to be informed of the addressees. Provision should be made for a remedy, if need be with the supervisory authority specified in principle 8 below. The cost of any rectification shall be borne by the person responsible for the file. It is desirable that the provisions of this principle should apply to everyone, irrespective of nationality or place of residence.

5. Principal of Non-discrimination

Subject to cases of exceptions restrictively envisaged under principle 6, data likely to give rise to unlawful or arbitrary discrimination, including information on racial or ethnic origin, colour, sex life, political opinions, religious, philosophical and other beliefs as well as membership of an association or trade union, should not be compiled.

6. Power to make Exceptions

Departures from principles 1 to 4 may be authorized only if they are necessary to protect national security, public order, public health or morality, as well as, *inter alia*, the rights and freedoms of others, especially persons being persecuted (humanitarian clause) provided that such departures are expressly specified in a law or equivalent regulation promulgated in accordance with the internal legal system which expressly states their limits and sets forth appropriate safeguards.

Exceptions to principle 5 relating to the prohibition of discrimination, in addition to being subject to the same safeguards as those prescribed for exceptions to principles 1 and 4, may be authorized only within the limits prescribed by the International Bill of Human Rights and the other relevant instruments in the field of protection of human rights and the prevention of discrimination.

7. Principle of Security

Appropriate measures should be taken to protect the files against both natural dangers, such as accidental loss or destruction and human dangers, such as unauthorized access, fraudulent misuse of data or contamination by computer viruses.

8. Supervision and Sanctions

The law of every country shall designate the authority which, in accordance with its domestic legal system, is to be responsible for supervising observance of the principles set forth above. This authority shall offer guarantees of impartiality, independence vis-à-vis persons or agencies responsible for processing and establishing data, and technical competence. In the event of violation of the provisions of the national law implementing the aforementioned principles, criminal or other penalties should be envisaged together with the appropriate individual remedies.

9.   Transborder Data Flows

When the legislation of two or more countries concerned by a transborder data flow offers comparable safeguards for the protection of privacy, information should be able to circulate as freely as inside each of the territories concerned. If there are no reciprocal safeguards, limitations on such circulation may not be imposed unduly and only in so far as the protection of privacy demands.

10.   Field of Application

The present principles should be made applicable, in the first instance, to all public and private computerized files as well as, by means of optional extension and subject to appropriate adjustments, to manual files. Special provision, also optional, might be made to extend all or part of the principles to files on legal persons particularly when they contain some information on individuals.

B.   *Application of the guidelines to personal data files kept by governmental international organizations*

The present guidelines should apply to personal data files kept by governmental international organizations, subject to any adjustments required to take account of any differences that might exist between files for internal purposes such as those that concern personnel management and files for external purposes concerning third parties having relations with the organization.

Each organization should designate the authority statutorily competent to supervise the observance of these guidelines.

Humanitarian clause: a derogation from these principles may be specifically provided for when the purpose of the file is the protection of human rights and fundamental freedoms of the individual concerned or humanitarian assistance.

A similar derogation should be provided in national legislation for governmental international organizations whose headquarters agreement does not preclude the implementation of the said national legislation as well as for non-governmental international organizations to which this law is applicable.

Human Rights and Scientific and Technological Developments

Guidelines for the regulation of computerized personal data files

I. Introduction

1. At its fortieth session, the Sub-Commission on Prevention of Discrimination and Protection of Minorities, by its resolution 1988/ 29 of 1 September 1988, and subsequently the Commission on Human Rights, by its resolution 1989/43 of 6 March 1989, considered the draft guidelines for the regulation of computerized personal data files submitted by the Special Rapporteur, Mr Louis Joinet, and contained in his final report (E/CN.4/Sub.2/1988/22).

2. On the recommendation of the Commission on Human Rights, the Economic and Social Council, by its resolution 1989/78 of 24 May 1989, decided to transmit to the General Assembly the final report by the Special Rapporteur (E/CN.4/Sub.2/1988/22) and requested the Secretary-General to bring that report to the attention of all Governments and to invite them to communicate their comments to him before 1 September 1989. The Council also requested the Secretary-General to submit to the Assembly for consideration at its forty-fourth session the final report of the Special Rapporteur and a report containing the views expressed thereon by Governments, and recommended that the Assembly consider, as a matter of priority, the adoption and publication of the guidelines on the use of computerized personal files.

3. Subsequently, a note verbale was sent to all Governments requesting them to submit their comments on the draft guidelines.

4. As at 20 September 1989, replies had been received from the following Governments: Burundi, Germany, Federal Republic of,

Japan, Netherlands, Norway, Sweden, United Kingdom of Great Britain and Northern Ireland.

5.   The present report summarizes in an analytical way the comments received by the above-mentioned Governments. Any further comments will be contained in addenda to the present report.

6.   The final report of the Special Rapporteur (E/CN.4/Sub.2/1988/22) is contained in the annex to the present report.

II.   General Comments and Suggestions

7.   The Governments of Burundi, Norway and Sweden expressed the view that the proposed guidelines for the regulation of computerized personal data files were well suited for their purpose and that the stated principles were basic for the protection of the human rights of privacy and freedom.

8.   In the view of Burundi and Norway, the necessity of elaborating an international instrument was highly desirable as safeguards because of the extensive increase of transborder data flows.

9.   Norway also noted that the consignment of data to the archives should not endanger a person's 'right to oblivion'. One must therefore ensure that the data from archives were not used again by any administrative agency or by others as a basis of decisions or for publication, without the consent of the person involved.

10.   The Government of the Netherlands stated that it was most interested in the final text of the draft guidelines and was pleased to note that account had been taken on various points of the observations made by the Netherlands in respect of a previous version of the guidelines.

11.   The Government of Japan pointed out that, since measures for the protection of personal information are different in each country because of their respective domestic legal systems, national sensibilities, and social, cultural and traditional backgrounds, the guidelines should be of such a nature and have a degree of flexibility as to permit each country to introduce its own domestic rules and regulations, which it deems most appropriate, taking into careful consideration such factors as domestic social characteristics of the individual country.

12.   Proceeding from that, Japan considered that the following should be stipulated in the instrument:

'(a)   These guidelines impose no legal obligations on States;

'(b)   The ways and means of how to implement these guidelines should be left to the discretion of each State.'

III.   Comments and Proposals in respect of Principles stating the Minimum Guarantees to be incorporated into National Legislation

A.   *Principle of lawfulness and fairness*

13.   Regarding principle (1) (appendix 1), on lawfulness and fairness, in the guidelines (see annex), no comments have been received.

B.   *Principle of accuracy*

14.   With regard to principle (2), on accuracy, in the guidelines, the United Kingdom held the view that a requirement for regular checks on the accuracy and relevance of files for their updating regularly, or whenever information was used, was too specific and procedurally exacting a requirement for an international instrument. It should be sufficient to state the underlying requirements that personal data should be accurate, kept up to date where necessary and relevant to the purpose for which the data is gathered. National jurisdictions should be left to decide how to give effect to these requirements in statutory and administrative terms. The United Kingdom agrees with the objections to the notion on the International Court of Justice of 'completeness' contained in paragraph 14 of the final report.

15.   Japan proposed the following wording of that principle:

'Persons responsible for the compilation of files or those responsible for keeping them should make an effort to conduct, with the purpose of keeping the data, regular checks on the accuracy and relevance of the data recorded and to ensure that they are kept up to date regularly or when the information contained in a file is used.'

C.   *Principle of purpose-specification*

16.   Concerning principle (3), on purpose-specification, the Federal Republic of Germany pointed out the following:

The requirement that the purpose of a file be made publicly known before it is established is not envisaged in either the Council of Europe's Convention of 28 January 1981 for the Protection of Individuals with Regard to Automatic Processing of Personal Data or the guidelines of the Organization for Economic Co-operation and Development (OECD) of 23 September 1980 governing the protection of privacy and transborder flows of personal data. On the other hand, one should lay down in principle 3 of the draft guidelines not only the principle of purpose-specification, which is reflected in the first half of article 8 b of the said data protection convention, but also everyone's right to ascertain the existence of a file and its main purposes, along the lines of article 8a of that Convention. The first sentence of principle 3 should therefore read as follows:

'The purpose which a file is to serve should be specified, legitimate and ascertainable to everyone before it is established, in order to make it possible subsequently to ensure that' ...

17.   Japan suggested to add the following words at the end of subparagraph 3(b):

In cases where personal data is used or disclosed for a distinct purpose, such as public service, in accordance with the domestic laws and regulations, without prejudicing unduly the rights or interests of the persons concerned or of third persons, such usage or disclosure of the data is not prohibited.

18.   Norway found the content of the principle to be satisfactory. It felt, however, that if a persons's consent was impossible to obtain, it might be useful to give a competent national body an authorization to give dispensations. In its view, the suggestion made by the Netherlands and contained in paragraph 15 of the final report would 'make it too easy to evade the guidelines'.

19.   With reference to the second line of principle (3), the United Kingdom considered the word 'when' to be preferable to the word 'before'.

D.   *Principle of interested-person access*

20.   In connection with principle (4), on interested-person access, the Government of Japan considered that the question that non-resident persons of a foreign nationality in a State be allowed access was a matter of the legislative policy of that State. Therefore, it is not appropriate to include it as a minimum rule in the proposed guidelines. For this reason, amendments should be made so that this paragraph simply implies the aim or endeavour.

21.   The Government of the United Kingdom noted that the penultimate sentence is vague. In its view, it ought to be made clear that remedies should be available for breach of any of the provisions described in the preceding sentence.

E.   *Principle of non-discrimination*

22.   With reference to principle (5), on non-discrimination, the Netherlands stated as follows:

> Principle 5 contains an express prohibition on the compilation of certain data, except where principle 6 permits exceptions to be made. The scope of this prohibition is not entirely clear. For example, the question arises of whether the compilation of the data in question under circumstances which could give rise to unlawful or arbitrary discrimination is meant, or the compilation of such data irrespective of the circumstances under which this is done. If the latter were the case, the provision would appear to be too broad in its scope because it would then cover cases in which there is no risk of discrimination at all. For example, there is no reason to place restrictions on political parties, trades unions, religious associations and so on establishing records of their members. The Government of the Netherlands feels there is a need to clarify this issue.

23.   In the view of the Federal Republic of Germany, principle (5) should be phrased as follows:

> Data likely to give rise to unlawful or arbitrary discrimination, especially information on racial or ethnic origin, colour, sex-life, political opinions, religious, philosophical and other beliefs, as well as membership of an association or a trade union, should not be compiled.
> Compilation is permitted by way of exception if the person concerned has given his consent or if compilation is necessary for the sake of the general public or a third party and the person concerned has no protectible interest in compilation being excluded, taking due account of the International Bill of Human Rights[1] and other relevant instruments in the field of protection of human rights and the prevention of discrimination.
> Even if these requirements are met, compilation is impermissible if national law does not guarantee adequate protection against discrimination.

24.   The same government further noted that the resultant need for legislation on a case-by-case basis is not feasible in view of the diverse situations covered that cannot be individually delimited. It is therefore essential to delimit in the principle itself the requisite exceptions and the criteria permitting the compilation of data, with

these criteria not being alterable at the national level. The requirement that the compilation of data be in the interest of the general
public or a third party and that protectible interests of the person
concerned be taken into account meets the conditions laid down by
the Federal Constitutional Court in its judgements concerning the
limitation of the right to self-determination in respect of personal
data. The restrictions now included in principle 5 have the same
substance as those originally envisaged in principle 6.

25.   Concerning principle (5), the Government of Japan made the
following comments:

> The guidelines itemize racial or ethnic origin, colour, sex-life, political
> opinions, religious, philosophical and other beliefs, as well as mem-
> bership of an association or a trade union as information that should
> not be recorded, but it is not appropriate to specify those items to be
> applicable in common to all States, because data falling under the
> sensitive category may differ among States and individuals. There-
> fore, this is a matter on which a decision should be made by each State
> in accordance with its traditions, the needs of its administrative public
> services and other relevant circumstances.

26.   According to the view of the United Kingdom, the opening
phrase would be clearer if it read 'Subject to the exceptions provided
for in principle (6) ...'

F.   *Power to make exceptions*

27.   The Federal Republic of Germany pointed out that taking into
account its amendment to principle (5), the requirement in the second paragraph of principle (6) in the draft guidelines that any exceptions be restricted by the provisions of the International Bill of
Human Rights and similar instruments is now met by weighing the
interests of the general public or a third party, on the one hand, and
the protectible interests of the person concerned, on the other. That
paragraph can therefore be dispensed with.

28.   Japan stated that the guidelines allowed exclusion from the
application of the principles given therein only in respect of national
security, public order, public health or morality or the rights and
freedoms of others. As the sort of files that are to be given exemption
from the application may differ from State to State, depending on
legislative judgements or other circumstances of the particular State
regarding the matter, it considered that the kind of files to be granted
exemption ought to be specified by each State according to its own

criteria. That view should be clearly stated. Japan was also of the view that the words 'criminal search' should be excluded from the application of the principles.

29.   The United Kingdom noted that the wording of the principle was very close to that of the Council of Europe Convention, and the United Kingdom would be content with it.

G.   *Principle of security*

30.   Norway and the United Kingdom expressed their consent with the content and wording of principle (7) on security.

H.   *Supervision and penalties*

31.   The Government of Norway considers that, relating to principle (8), 'the goal must be to establish an authority with the greatest possible independence of the Government'.

32.   In the view of the Government of the Federal Republic of Germany, 'the authority to be set up to supervize observance of the principles contained in the guidelines should be not only impartial, but also independent of the bodies responsible for keeping the files'.

33.   Japan noted that what was important was how to secure the implementation of the guidelines and the appropriate measures. Whether criminal penalties should be imposed or not should be decided in accordance with the domestic law of each State.

34.   The Government of the United Kingdom is of the opinion that the last sentence of the text would be clarified by saying '... principles, criminal penalties and individual remedies should be available'.

I.   *Transborder data flows*

35.   The Government of the United Kingdom suggested the following amendments to the text of the principle: in the second line, the words 'more or less equivalent' would be better expressed as 'comparable'. The last sentence would be better expressed thus by: 'If there are no comparable safeguards, limitations on such flows should not be unduly imposed and then only in so far as the protection of privacy requires'. The United Kingdom noted that it was content that the protection of privacy should be the only criterion mentioned in the last sentence of the text.

J.   *Field of application*

36.   According to the Norwegian reply, the rules should cover computerized as well as manual files and legal persons should also be protected by the privacy legislation.

37.   The Government of Sweden is of the view that the clause concerning principle (10) is to be understood as relating to primarily computerized files, whether public or private. As far as manual files are concerned, the clause is to be understood as though the principles of the proposed guidelines are applicable only to such files when compiled and kept for the purpose of compiling and keeping computerized files.

38.   The Federal Republic of Germany pointed out that in the explanations on the guidelines it should be made clear that 'manual file' was to be understood to mean a manually kept data file and not a conventional office file.

39.   The Government of the United Kingdom considered that, as it is made clear in their title, these guidelines relate to computerized personal data files. Manual files and non-personal data lie outside the terms of reference and this article should not introduce them. On the substance, the United Kingdom could not in any case accept that the principles of individual privacy should apply to non-personal data; manual files would be very expensive to cover by such measures and extension of the principles to them should at the most be optional, and such issues as access to manual files would in any case need to be considered separately in the context of freedom of information. As regards the last sentence of the text, it was of the view that the words 'if requested' were unclear (requested by whom?); and, in any case, the sentence should be rephrased to make it clear that States had the option if they wished of extending the principles to cover files on legal persons when they contained some information on individuals.

40.   Japan is of the view that manual files should be excluded from the application of the guidelines, or the decision on this application should be entrusted to each State. It may take much time to search manual files and consequently that would place a great burden on the authorities.

K. *Application of the guidelines to personal data files kept by governmental international organizations*

41. The Government of Norway is of the opinion that international organizations filing sensitive data, should follow the rules of the guidelines, and should register in the United Nations, stating that they would follow the principles in the guidelines. According to the same view, an authority to supervise the observance of the guidelines should be within the United Nations.

Note

1 Comprising the Universal Declaration of Human Rights (General Assembly resolution 217 A (III), the International Covenant on Economic, Social and Cultural Rights and the International Covenant on Civil and Political Rights and the Optional Protocol thereto (General Assembly resolution 2200 A (XXI), annex).

Appendix 4: European Community Modified Proposal

Modified proposal for a Council Directive on the protection of individuals with regard to the processing of personal data and to the free movement of such data

The Council of the European Communities,

Having regard to the Treaty establishing the European Economic Community and in particular Articles 100a and 113 thereof.

Having regard to the proposal from the Commission,

in cooperation with the European Parliament,

Having regard to the opinion of the Economic and Social Committee,

(1)   Whereas the objectives of the Community, as laid down in the Treaty as amended by the Single European Act, include establishing an ever closer union among the peoples of Europe, fostering closer relations between the States belonging to the Community, ensuring economic and social progress by common action to eliminate the barriers which divide Europe, encouraging the constant improvement of the living conditions of its peoples, preserving and strengthening peace and liberty and promoting democracy on the basis of the fundamental rights recognized in the constitutions and laws of the Member States and in the European Convention for the Protection of Human Rights and Fundamental Freedoms;

(2)   Whereas the establishment and the functioning of an internal market in which, in accordance with Article 8a of the Treaty, the free movement of goods, persons, services and capital is ensured require not only that personal data should be able to flow freely, regardless

of in which Member States they are processed or requested, but also that fundamental rights should be safeguarded;

(3)   Whereas the internal market comprises an area without frontiers; whereas, for that reason, the national authorities in the various Member States are increasingly being called upon, by virtue of the operation of Community law, to collaborate and exchange personal data so as to be able to perform their duties or carry out tasks on behalf of an authority in another Member State;

(4)   Whereas the increase in scientific and technical cooperation and the coordinated introduction of new telecommunications networks in the Community necessitate and facilitate cross-border flows of personal data;

(5)   Whereas the difference in levels of protection of privacy in relation to the processing of personal data afforded in the Member States may constitute an obstacle to flows of such data and distort competition; whereas this difference in levels of protection is due to the existence of a wide variety of laws, regulations and administrative provisions;

(6)   Whereas in order to remove the obstacles to flows of personal data, the level of protection of privacy in relation to the processing of such data must be equivalent in all the Member States; whereas to that end it is necessary to approximate the relevant laws;

(7)   Whereas the object of the national laws on the processing of personal data is to protect fundamental rights, notably the right to privacy recognized also in Article 8 of the Convention for the Protection of Human Rights and Fundamental Freedoms and in the general principles of Community law; whereas, for that reason, the approximation of those laws must not result in any lessening of the protection they afford but must, on the contrary, seek to ensure a high level of protection in the Community;

(8)   Whereas the principles underlying the protection of privacy in relation to the processing of personal data set forth in this Directive may be supplemented or clarified, in particular as far as certain sectors are concerned, by specific rules based on those principles;

(9)   Whereas the protection principles must apply to all data files where the activities of the controller of the file are governed by Community law; whereas public-sector files which are not governed by Community law should, as is provided for in the resolution of the

representatives of the Governments of the Member States of the European Communities meeting within the Council of ..., be subject to the same protection principles set forth in national laws; whereas, however, data files falling exclusively within the confines of the exercise of a natural person's right to privacy, such as personal address files, must be excluded;

(10)   Whereas any processing of personal data in the Community should be carried out in accordance with the law of the Member State in which the data file is located so that individuals are not deprived of the protection to which they are entitled under this Directive; whereas, in this connection, each part of a data file divided among several Member States must be considered a separate data file and transfer to a non-member country must not be a bar to such protection;

(11)   Whereas any processing of personal data must be lawful; whereas such lawfulness must be based on the consent of the data subject or on Community or national law;

(12)   Whereas national laws may, under the conditions laid down in this Directive, specify rules on the lawfulness of processing; whereas, however, such a possibility cannot serve as a basis for supervision by a Member State other than the State in which the data file is located, the obligation on the part of the latter to ensure, in accordance with this Directive, the protection of privacy in relation to the processing of personal data being sufficient, under Community law, to permit the free flow of data;

(13)   Whereas the procedures of notification, in respect of public- or private-sector data files, and provision of information at the time of first communication, in respect of private-sector data files, are designed to ensure the transparency essential to the exercise by the data subject of the right of access to data relating to him;

(14)   Whereas the data subject must, if his consent is to be valid and when data relating to him are collected from him, be given accurate and full information;

(15)   Whereas the data subject must be able to exercise the right of access in order to verify the lawfulness of the processing of data relating to him and their quality;

(16)   Whereas, if data are to be processed, they must fulfil certain requirements; whereas the processing of data which are capable by their very nature of infringing the right to privacy must be prohib-

172   *Appendices*

ited unless the data subject gives his explicit consent; whereas, however, on important public interest grounds, notably in relation to the medical profession, derogations may be granted on the basis of a law laying down precisely and strictly the conditions governing and limits to the processing of this type of data;

(17)   Whereas the protection of privacy in relation to personal data requires that appropriate security measures be taken, both at the level of design and at that of the techniques of processing, to prevent any unauthorized processing;

(18)   Whereas as regards the media the Member States may grant derogations from the provisions of this Directive in-so-far as they are designed to reconcile the right to privacy with the freedom of information and the right to receive and impart information, as guaranteed notably in Article 10 of the Convention for the Protection of Human Rights and Fundamental Freedoms;

(19)   Whereas the Member States must encourage the drawing-up, by the business circles concerned, of European codes of conduct or professional ethics relating to certain specific sectors; whereas the Commission will support such initiatives and will take them into account when it considers the appropriateness of new, specific measures in respect of certain sectors;

(20)   Whereas, in the event of non-compliance with this Directive, liability in any action for damages must rest with the controller of the file; whereas dissuasive sanctions must be applied in order to ensure effective protection;

(21)   Whereas it is also necessary that the transfer of personal data should be able to take place with third countries having an adequate level of protection; whereas, in the absence of such protection in third countries, this Directive provides, in particular, for negotiation procedures with those countries;

(22)   Whereas the principles contained in this Directive concretize and amplify those contained in the Council of European Convention of 28 January 1981 for the Protection of individuals with regard to Automatic Processing of Personal Data;

(23)   Whereas the existence in each Member State of an independent supervisory authority is an essential component of the protection of individuals in relation to the processing of personal data; whereas a similar function must be performed at Community level by a Com-

mittee on the Protection of Personal Data set up to advise the Commission and contribute to the uniform application of the national rules adopted pursuant to this Directive; whereas to that end it must be composed of representatives of the national supervisory authorities and be completely independent in the performance of its functions;

(24) Whereas the adoption of additional measures for applying the principles set forth in this Directive calls for the conferment of rule-making powers on the Commission and the establishment of an Advisory Committee in accordance with the procedures laid down in Council Decision 87/373/EEC of 13 July 1987.

Has adopted this Directive:

Chapter I General Provisions

Article 1 *Object of the Directive*

1. The Member States shall ensure, in accordance with this Directive, the protection of the privacy of individuals in relation to the processing of personal data contained in data files.

2. The Member States shall neither restrict nor prohibit the free flow of personal data between Member States for reasons to do with the protection afforded under to paragraph 1.

Article 2 *Definitions*

For the purposes of this Directive:

(a) 'personal data' means any information relating to an identified or identifiable individual ('data subject'); an identifiable individual is notably an individual who can be identified by reference to an identification number or a similar identifying particular;

(b) 'depersonalize' means modify personal data in such a way that the information they contain can no longer be associated with a specified or specifiable individual except at the price of an excessive effort in terms of staff, expenditure and time;

(c) 'personal data file' (file) means any set of personal data, whether centralized or geographically dispersed, undergoing automatic

processing or which, although not undergoing automatic processing, are structured and accessible in an organized collection
according to specific criteria in such a way as to facilitate their
use or combination;

(d) 'processing' means the following operations, whether or not
performed by automated means: the recording, storage or combination of data, and their alteration, use or communication,
including transmission, dissemination, retrieval, blocking and
erasure;

(e) 'controller of the file' means the natural or legal person, public
authority, agency or other body competent under Community
law or the national law of a Member State to decide what will be
the purpose of the file, which categories of personal data will be
stored, which operations will be applied to them and which
third parties may have access;

(f) 'supervisory authority' means the independent public authority
or other independent body designated by each Member State in
accordance with Article 26 of this Directive;

(g) 'public sector' means all the authorities, organizations and entities of a Member State that are governed by public law, with the
exception of those which carry on an industrial or commercial
activity, and bodies and entities governed by private law where
they take part in the exercise of official authority;

(h) 'private sector' means any natural or legal person or association, including public-sector authorities, organizations and entities in so far as they carry on an industrial or commercial activity.

Article 3 Scope

1.   The Member States shall apply this Directive to files in the public
and private sectors with the exception of files in the public sector
where the activities of that sector do not fall within the scope of
Community law.

2.   This Directive shall not apply to files held by:

(a)   an individual solely for private and personal purposes; or

(b) non-profit-making political, philosophical, religious, cultural, trade-union, sporting or leisure bodies as part of their legitimate aims, on condition that they relate only to those members and corresponding members who have consented to being included therein and that they are not communicated to third parties.

Article 4   Law applicable

1. Each Member State shall apply this Directive to:

(a) all files located in its territory;

(b) the controller of a file resident in its territory who uses from its territory a file located in a third country whose law does not provide an adequate level of protection, unless such use is only sporadic.

2. Each Member State shall apply Articles 5, 6, 8, 9, 10, 17, 18 and 21 of this Directive to a user consulting a file located in a third country from a terminal located in the territory of a Member State, unless such use is only sporadic.

3. Where a file is moved temporarily from one Member State to another Member State, the latter shall place no obstacle in the way and shall not require the completion of any formalities over and above those applicable in the Member State in which the file is normally located.

Chapter II   Lawfulness of Processing in the Public Sector

Article 5   Principles

1. Subject to Article 6, the Member States shall, with respect to files in the public sector, provide in their law that:

(a) the creation of a file and any other processing of personal data shall be lawful in so far as they are necessary for the performance of the tasks of the public authority in control of the file;

(b) the processing of data for a purpose other than that for which the file was created shall be lawful if:
  – the data subject consents thereto; or
  – it is effected on the basis of Community law, or of a law, or a measure taken pursuant to a law, of a Member State con-

forming with this Directive which authorizes it and defines the limits thereto; or
- the legitimate interests of the data subject do not preclude such change of purpose; or
- it is necessary in order to ward off an imminent threat to public order or a serious infringement of the rights of others.

Article 6   Processing in the public sector having as its object the communication of personal data

1.   The Member States shall provide in their law that the communication of personal data contained in the files of a public-sector entity shall be lawful only if:

(a)   It is necessary for the performance of the tasks of the public-sector entity communicating or requesting communication of the data; or

(b)   It is requested by a natural or legal person in the private sector who invokes a legitimate interest, on condition that the interest of the data subject does not prevail.

2.   Without prejudice to paragraph 1, the Member States may specify the conditions under which the communication of personal data is lawful.

3.   The Member States shall provide in their law that, in the circumstances referred to in paragraph 1(b), the controller of the file shall inform data subjects of the communication of personal data. The Member States may provide for the replacing of such provision of information by prior authorization by the supervisory authority.

Article 7   Obligation to notify the supervisory authority

1.   The Member States shall provide in their law that the creation of a public-sector file the personal data in which might be communicated shall be notified in advance to the supervisory authority and recorded in a register kept by that authority. The register shall be freely available for consultation.

2.   The Member States shall specify the information which must be notified to the supervisory authority. That information shall include at least the name and address of the controller of the file, the purpose of the file, a description of the types of data it contains, the third

parties to whom the data might be communicated and a description of the measures taken pursuant to Article 18.

3.   The Member States may provide that paragraphs 1 and 2 shall apply to other public-sector files and that consultation of the register may be restricted for the reasons stated in Article 15(1).

Chapter III   Lawfulness of Processing in the Private Sector

Article 8   Principles

1.   The Member States shall provide in their law that, without the consent of the data subject, the recording in a file and any other processing of personal data shall be lawful only if it is effected in accordance with this Directive and if:

(a)   the processing is carried out under a contract, or in the context of a quasi-contractual relationship of trust, with the data subject and is necessary for their discharge; or

(b)   the data come from sources generally accessible to the public and their processing is intended solely for correspondence purposes; or

(c)   the controller of the file is pursuing a legitimate interest, on condition that the interest of the data subject does not prevail.

2.   The Member States shall provide in their law that it shall be for the controller of the file to ensure that no communication is incompatible with the purpose of the file or is contrary to public policy. In the event of on-line consultation, the same obligations shall be incumbent on the user.

3.   Without prejudice to paragraph 1, the Member States may specify the conditions under which the processing of personal data is lawful.

Article 9   Obligation to inform the data subject

1.   The Member States shall, with respect to the private sector, provide in their law that at the time of first communication or of the affording of an opportunity for on-line consultation the controller of the file shall inform the data subject accordingly, indicating also the purpose of the file, the types of data stores therein and his name and address.

2.   The provision of information under paragraph 1 shall not be mandatory in the circumstances referred to in Article 8(1)(b). There shall be no obligation to inform where communication is required by law.

3.   If the data subject objects to communication or any other processing, the controller of the file shall cease the processing objected to unless he is authorized by law to carry it out.

Article 10   Exceptions to the obligation to inform the data subject

If major practical difficulties, overriding legitimate interests of the controller of the file or a similar interest of a third party stand in the way of informing the data subject as provided for in Article 9(1), the Member States may provide in their law that the supervisory authority may authorize a derogation.

Article 11   Obligation to notify the supervisory authority

1.   The Member States shall provide in their law that the controller of the file shall notify the creation of a personal data file where the data are intended to be communicated and do not come from sources generally accessible to the public. The notification shall be made to the supervisory authority of the Member State in which the file is located or, if it is not located in a Member State, to the supervisory authority of the Member State in which the controller of the file resides. The controller of the file shall notify to the competent national authorities any change in the purpose of the file or any change of address.

2.   The Member States shall specify the information which must be notified to the supervisory authority. That information shall include at least the name and address of the controller of the file, the purpose of the file, a description of the types of data it contains, the third parties to whom the data might be communicated and a description of the measures taken pursuant to Article 18.

3.   The Member States may provide that paragraphs 1 and 2 shall apply to other private-sector files and that the information referred to in paragraph 2 shall be accessible to the public.

Chapter IV   Rights of Data Subjects

Article 12   Informed consent

Any giving of consent by a data subject to the processing of personal data relating to him within the meaning of this Directive shall be valid only if:

(a)   the data subject is supplied with the following information:
  - the purposes of the file and the types of data stored;
  - the type of use and, where appropriate, the recipients of the personal data contained in the file;
  - the name and address of the controller of the file;

(b)   it is specific and express and specifies the types of data, forms of processing and potential recipients covered by it;

(c)   it may be withdrawn by the data subject at any time without retroactive effect.

Article 13   Provision of information at the time of collection

1.   The Member States shall guarantee individuals from whom personal data are collected the right to be informed at least about:

(a)   the purposes of the file for which the information is intended; and

(b)   the obligatory or voluntary nature of their reply to the questions to which answers are sought; and

(c)   the consequences if they fail to reply; and

(d)   the recipients of the information; and

(e)   the existence of the right of access to and rectification of the data relating to them; and

(f)   the name and address of the controller of the file.

2.   Paragraph 1 shall not apply to the collection of information where to inform the data subject would prevent the exercise of the supervision and verification functions of a public authority or the maintenance of public order.

Article 14   Additional rights of data subjects

The Member States shall grant a data subject the following rights:

1.   To oppose, for legitimate reasons, the processing of personal data relating to him.

2.   Not to be subject to an administrative or private decision involving an assessment of his conduct which has as its sole basis the automatic processing of personal data defining his profile or personality.

3.   To know of the existence of a file and to know its main purposes and the identity and habitual residence, headquarters or place of business of the controller of the file.

4.   To obtain at reasonable intervals and without excessive delay or expense confirmation of whether personal data relating to him are stored in a file and communication to him of such data in an intelligible form. The Member States may provide that the right of access to medical data may be exercised only through a doctor.

5.   To obtain, as the case may be, rectification, erasure or blocking of such data if they have been processed in violation of the provisions of this Directive.

6.   To obtain upon request and free of charge the erasure of data relating to him held in files used for market research or advertising purposes.

7.   To obtain, in the event of the application of paragraph 5 and if the data have been communicated to third parties, notification to the latter of the rectification, erasure or blocking.

8.   To have a judicial remedy if the rights guaranteed in this Article are infringed.

Article 15   Exceptions to the data subject's right of access to public-sector files

1.   The Member States may limit by statute the rights provided for in paragraphs 3 and 4 of Article 14 for reasons relating to:
(a)   national security, or
(b)   defence, or
(c)   criminal proceedings, or
(d)   public safety, or
(e)   a substantial economic and financial interest of a Member State or of the European Communities, or
(f)   the need for the public authorities to perform monitoring or inspection functions, or
(g)   an equivalent right of another individual and the rights and freedoms of others.

2.   In the circumstances referred to in paragraph 1, the supervisory authority shall be empowered to carry out, at the request of the data subject, the necessary checks on the file.

3.   The Member States may place limits on the data subject's right of access to data compiled temporarily for the purpose of extracting statistical information therefrom.

Chapter V   Data Quality

Article 16   Principles

1.   The Member States shall provide that personal data shall be:

(a)   collected and processed fairly and lawfully;

(b)   stored for specified, explicit and lawful purposes and used in a way compatible with those purposes;

(c)   adequate, relevant and not excessive in relation to the purposes for which they are stored;

(d)   accurate and, if necessary, kept up to date; inaccurate or incomplete data shall be erased or rectified;

(e)   kept in a form which permits identification of the data subjects for no longer than is necessary for the purpose for which the data are stored.

2.   It shall be for the controller of the file to ensure that paragraph 1 is complied with.

Article 17   Special categories of data

1.   The Member States shall prohibit, without the express and written consent, freely given, of the data subject, the automatic processing of data revealing racial origin, political opinions, religious or philosophical beliefs or trade-union membership, and of data concerning health or sexual life.

2.   The Member States may, on important public interest grounds, grant derogations from paragraph 1 on the basis of a law specifying the types of data which may be stored and the persons who may

have access to the file and providing suitable safeguards against abuse and unauthorized access.

3.   Data concerning criminal convictions shall be held only in public-sector files.

Article 18   Data security

1.   The Member States shall provide in their law that the controller of a file shall take appropriate technical and organizational measures to protect personal data stored in the file against accidental or unauthorized destruction or accidental loss and against unauthorized access, modification or other processing.

Such measures shall ensure in respect of automated files an appropriate level of security having regard to the state of the art in this field, the cost of taking the measures, the nature of the data to be protected and the assessment of the potential risks. To that end, the controller of the file shall take into consideration any recommendations on data security and network interoperability formulated by the Commission in accordance with the procedure provided for in Article 29.

2.   Methods guaranteeing adequate security shall be chosen for the transmission of personal data in a network.

3.   In the event of on-line consultation, the hardware and software shall be designed in such a way that the consultation takes place within the limits of the authorization granted by the controller of the file.

4.   The obligations referred to in paragraphs 1 to 3 shall also be incumbent on persons who, either *de facto* or by contract, control the operations relating to a file.

5.   Any person who in the course of his work has access to information contained in files shall not communicate it to third parties without the agreement of the controller of the file.

Chapter VI Provisions Specifically Relating to Certain Sectors

Article 19

The Member States may grant in respect of the press, radio and television derogations from the provisions of this Directive in so far as they are necessary to reconcile the right to privacy with the rules governing freedom of information and of the press.

Article 20

The Member States shall encourage the business circles concerned to participate in drawing up European codes of conduct or professional ethics in respect of certain sectors on the basis of the principles set forth in this Directive.

Chapter VII Liability and Sanctions

Article 21 Liability

1. The Member States shall provide in their law that any individual whose personal data have been stored in a file and who suffers damage as a result of processing or of any act incompatible with this Directive shall be entitled to compensation from the controller of the file.

2. The Member States may provide that the controller of the file shall not be liable for any damage resulting from the loss or destruction of data or from unauthorized access if he proves that he has taken appropriate measures to fulfil the requirements of Articles 18 and 22.

Article 22 Processing on behalf of the controller of the file

1. The Member States shall provide in their law that the controller of the file must, where processing is carried out on his behalf, ensure that the necessary security and organizational measures are taken and choose a person or enterprise who provides sufficient guarantees in that respect.

2. Any person who collects or processes personal data on behalf of the controller of the file shall fulfil the obligations provided for in Articles 16 and 18 of this Directive.

3.   The contract shall be in writing and shall stipulate, in particular, that the personal data may be divulged by the person providing the service or his employees only with the agreement of the controller of the file.

Article 23   Sanctions

Each Member State shall make provision in its law for the application of dissuasive sanctions in order to ensure compliance with the measures taken pursuant to this Directive.

Chapter VIII   Transfer of Personal Data to Third Countries

Article 24   Principles

1.   The Member States shall provide in their law that the transfer to a third country, whether temporary or permanent, of personal data which are undergoing processing or which have been gathered with a view to processing may take place only if that country ensures an adequate level of protection.

2.   The Member States shall inform the Commission of cases in which an importing third country does not ensure an adequate level of protection.

3.   Where the Commission finds, either on the basis of information supplied by Member States or on the basis of other information, that a third country does not have an adequate level of protection and that the resulting situation is likely to harm the interests of the Community or of a Member State, it may enter into negotiations with a view to remedying the situation.

4.   The Commission may decide, in accordance with the procedure laid down in Article 30 (2) of this Directive, that a third country ensures an adequate level of protection by reason of the international commitments it has entered into or of its domestic law.

5.   Measures taken pursuant to this Article shall be in keeping with the obligations incumbent on the Community by virtue of international agreements, both bilateral and multilateral, governing the protection of individuals in relation to the automatic processing of personal data.

Article 25   Derogation

1.   A Member State may derogate from Article 24(1) in respect of a given export on submission by the controller of the file of sufficient proof that an adequate level of protection will be provided. The Member State may grant a derogation only after it has informed the Commission and the Member States thereof and in the absence of notice of opposition given by a Member State or the Commission within a period of ten days.

2.   Where notice of opposition is given, the Commission shall adopt appropriate measures in accordance with the procedure laid down in Article 30(2).

Chapter IX   Supervisory Authorities and Committee on the Protection of Personal Data

Article 26   Supervisory authority

1.   The Member States shall set up an independent authority to supervise the protection of personal data. The authority shall monitor the application of the national measures taken pursuant to this Directive and perform all the functions that are entrusted to it by this Directive.

2.   The authority shall have investigative powers and effective powers of intervention against the creation and exploitation of files which do not conform with this Directive. To that end, it shall have, *inter alia*, the right of access to files covered by this Directive and shall be given the power to gather all the information necessary for the performance of its supervisory duties.

3.   The authority may consider any complaint by any individual in connection with the protection of individuals in relation to personal data.

Article 27   Committee on the Protection of Personal Data

1.   A Committee on the Protection of Personal Data is hereby set up. The Committee, which shall have advisory status and shall act independently, shall be composed of representatives of the supervisory authorities, provided for in Article 26, of all the Member States and shall be chaired by a representative of the Commission.

2.   The secretariat of the Committee on the Protection of Personal Data shall be provided by the Commission's departments.

3.   The Committee on the Protection of Personal Data shall adopt its own rules of procedure.

4.   The Committee on the Protection of Personal Data shall examine questions placed on the agenda by its Chairman, either on his own initiative or at the reasoned request of a representative of the supervisory authorities, and concerned with the application of the Community- law provisions on the protection of personal data.

Article 28   Tasks of the Committee on the Protection of Personal Data

1.   The Committee on the Protection of Personal Data shall:
(a)   contribute to the uniform application of the national rules adopted pursuant to this Directive;
(b)   assess the level of protection in the Community and in third countries;
(c)   advise the Commission on any draft additional or specific measures to be taken to safeguard the protection of privacy.

2.   If the Committee on the Protection of Personal Data finds that significant divergences are arising between the laws or practices of the Member States in relation to the protection of personal data which might affect the equivalence of protection in the Community, it shall inform the Commission accordingly.

3.   The Committee on the Protection of Personal Data may formulate recommendations on any questions concerning the protection of individuals in relation to personal data in the Community. The recommendations shall be recorded in the minutes and may be transmitted to the Advisory Committee referred to in Article 30. The Commission shall inform the Committee on the Protection of Personal Data of the action it has taken in response to the recommendations.

4.   The Committee on the Protection of Personal Data shall draw up an annual report on the situation regarding the protection of individuals in relation to the processing of personal data in the Community and in third countries, which it shall transmit to the European Parliament, the Council and the Commission.

Chapter X   Rule-Making Powers of the Commission

Article 29   *Exercise of rule-making powers*

The Commission shall, in accordance with the procedure laid down in Article 30(2), take such additional measures as are necessary to adapt the provisions of this Directive to the specific characteristics of certain sectors having regard to the state of the art in this field and to the codes of conduct.

Article 30   *Advisory Committee*

1.   The Commission shall be assisted by an Advisory Committee composed of representatives of the Member States and chaired by a representative of the Commission.

2.   The Commission representative shall submit to the Committee a draft of the measures to be taken. The Committee shall deliver its opinion on the draft within such period as the Chairman may fix in the light of the urgency of the matter under consideration, if necessary by taking a vote. The opinion shall be recorded in the minutes. In addition, each Member State shall be entitled to have its position recorded in the minutes. The Commission shall take the utmost account of the opinion delivered by the Committee. It shall inform the Committee of the manner in which its opinion has been taken into account.

Final Provisions

Article 31

1.   The Member States shall bring into force the laws, regulations and administrative provisions necessary for them to comply with this Directive 1 January 1993.

The provisions adopted pursuant to the first subparagraph shall make express reference to this Directive.

2.   The Member States shall communicate to the Commission the texts of the provisions of national law which they adopt in the field covered by this Directive.

Article 32

This Directive is addressed to the Member States.

Index